Plump Pups

AND

Fat Cats

Plump Pups

AND

Fat Cats

A Seven-Point Weight Loss Program
for Your Overweight Pet

Steve Duno

St. Martin's Griffin ❧ New York

Design by Nancy Resnick

Library of Congress Cataloging-in-Publication Data

Duno, Steve.

Plump pups and fat cats : a seven-point weight loss program for your overweight pet / Steve Duno. — 1st St. Martin's Griffin ed.

p.   cm.

ISBN 0-312-24436-3

1. Dogs—Diseases—Diet therapy. 2. Cats—Diseases—Diet therapy. 3. Dogs—Exercise. 4. Cats—Exercise. 5. Dogs—Health. 6. Cats—Health. 7. Obesity in animals. I. Title.

SF991.D8   1999
636.7' 089325—dc21   99-34014
                                                                CIP

First Edition: November 1999

10 9 8 7 6 5 4 3 2 1

This book is dedicated to my most beloved friends,
Nicki and Lou.

Contents

Acknowledgments

The creation, publication, and success of any book depends on more than just one person. Accordingly, I would like to thank those persons who helped me make this book possible. To my human spell checker and nitpicker Nicki Mason, thank you for staying up nights with pencil in hand. Thanks also to my editor, Heather Jackson, for all her help and guidance, and to Laura Peterson, my agent at Curtis Brown, for her skills and advice. Lastly, thanks to my family and friends for all their support and encouragement.

Steve Duno

Preface

More than at any other time in history, much of our world is experiencing a period of abundance. In the United States and Europe particularly, food is readily available, business is booming, and standards of living are on the rise.

Unfortunately, prosperity often leads to excess, especially with regard to eating habits. It's no secret that much of the population, adults and children alike, are substantially overweight, and getting more so. As lifestyles become less active and food more available, waistlines expand and fitness declines.

Just as we have allowed this problem to affect ourselves and our children, so too have we let it affect our pets. Dogs and cats are fast becoming as sedentary and overweight as their owners, leading to obesity and the medical and behavioral problems it causes.

During my years as an animal behaviorist, I've observed and worked with many overweight dogs and cats. Some of these animals suffered marked declines in mobility and overall health; many of them developed debilitating structural problems, while others were eventually diagnosed with more serious disorders such as diabetes, cardiovascular or respiratory disease, kidney or liver abnormalities, or even cancer—all directly or indirectly caused by their chronic obesity. With my help (and the help of a caring veterinarian), a good number of the owners of these unfortunate pets were able to gradually trim them down, usually resulting in better health and a happier pet.

You would think that, being professionally attuned to the health and well-being of dogs and cats, I would have noticed my own dog gaining weight. Wrong. Ironically, I fell victim to the same trap as so many other caring owners. During a six- or seven-month period of intense work on a book, my canine pal's slow weight gain escaped me. A fairly large dog to begin with, Louie (a Rottweiler mix) went from an optimal weight of seventy pounds to a hefty seventy-seven. Though not technically obese, a weight gain of 10 percent is not a healthy option for dog, cat, or human. It took an astutely observant good friend and fellow trainer to point out that Louie had become a bit "thick" of late. I was, of course, embarrassed and concerned. How could this have happened?

In my case (or, more accurately, Louie's), the answer was simple. At over nine years of age, Louie's metabolism had slowed considerably; he just wasn't burning calories as fast as he had just a year or two before. Once capable of maintaining his ideal weight on about three cups of food per day, his daily caloric expenditures had slowly decreased by about 10 percent over a six- or seven-month period, causing a corresponding weight increase. To compound matters, my hectic writing schedule had prevented me from exercising Louie as much as I might normally like. The combination of these two factors caused my buddy to lose his boyish figure.

Louie's weight problem was solved rather easily, I'm happy to say. We simply cut his caloric intake by about 10 percent and added an extra walk and play session each day. Now, about four months later, he is back to his ideal weight and is just as active as ever. The experience, however, got me thinking: If I could let my own dog gain weight, what about other less informed owners?

My experience with Louie, coupled with my observations of clients' pets, convinced me that this is a real problem that needs to be addressed. Too many cats and dogs are overweight, much to the chagrin of their owners, who often are not even aware of their pets' obesity. I've seen it time and again: A client will come to me with a behavioral pet problem, only to be shocked and embarrassed to learn that his or her pet is substantially overweight. Disobedient or destructive behavior, either aggressive food guarding or a compulsive fixation on food, is often directly linked to the excess weight. The extra weight will also often cause the dog or cat to act in a much more lethargic manner, resulting in a slower response to the owner's requests. When informed of the health risks that obesity subjects their dogs and cats to, the owners of these overweight animals almost always attempt to reform their pets' eating and exercise habits to save their loved ones from discomfort, depression, and poor health.

Plump Pups and Fat Cats: A Seven-Point Weight Loss Plan for Your Overweight Pet is my answer to the epidemic of pet obesity. Hundreds of diet and exercise books have been written to help humans in their never-ending quest to look good and feel healthy. Until now, not one has been written specifically for the cat or dog, despite the fact that the problem is severe and worsening.

The book explains in detail the causes of obesity and offers practical advice on how to remove and keep off health-sapping excess weight from your canine or feline companion. Numerous solutions to the problem are offered, including:

- adjustments in dietary habits
- the introduction of fun, natural exercise regimens tailored to the specific pet
- tips on teaching your pet tricks and agility work to help keep him interested and involved
- the initiation of environmental "enrichment" programs (adaptations to the pet's habitat that relieve boredom while increasing physical and mental activity levels)
- owner education on the perils of pet obesity
- good and bad feeding habits
- how to reward the pet with things other than food
- custom-tailoring a pet's lifestyle to match her unique metabolism

Plump Pups and Fat Cats contains other features that make it extremely effective. One is its ability to offer the reader more than just one solution to a problem. As with a human, each dog or cat is a unique individual who may respond better to one course of action than to another. Accordingly, the book provides numerous options in an attempt to customize an approach to the pet in question. No one diet works for all dogs; not every exercise appeals to all cats. For instance, a nine-year-old Maltese with a slowing metabolism might respond well to the owner simply feeding her less food. But a grossly overweight three-year-old Staffordshire bull terrier (a high-strung breed known for having a very high food drive) might become stressed over suddenly losing 20 or 30 percent of his beloved food, which could lead to unpredictable, undesirable behaviors. The owner of this pet might have better results switching the dog over to a less fattening food, one that would have the same volume but would contain fewer calories. The dog would still feel as if he were eating the same amount, and he would therefore not become stressed.

Another unique aspect of the book is its holistic approach to pet weight loss. Regulating diet and exercise, though key components in solving the problem, aren't the only factors involved. The overall health and happiness of the pet (or lack thereof) also plays a vital role in affecting weight loss or gain. Accordingly, the book offers tips on how to adjust a pet's environment and daily schedule to best ensure an involved, purposeful, happy lifestyle. Included in these tips are discussions on training, socialization, environmental enrichment, problem solving, and proper pet-owner relations.

The introduction identifies the causes and effects of obesity in dogs and cats, helping owners completely understand the problem and its consequences. The rest of the book details easy strategies that, if implemented, will result not only in significant weight loss for the pet, but also in improved health, behavior, and attitude. Specific information for dogs and cats is provided, as are unique breed recommendations where appropriate. The book concludes with a brief review of the seven key points to pet weight loss, and it strongly reinforces the suggestion put forth in the introduction about finding and utilizing the services of a competent, caring veterinarian—a key player in helping to reduce your pet's weight. A careful, concerted effort by you, the other family members, and your veterinarian, in conjunction with the information provided in this book, should succeed in helping your pet lose and keep off those unwanted pounds.

Plump Pups

AND

Fat Cats

Introduction

Why Do Our Pets Become Fat?

Ever see a fat wolf or a chunky cheetah? Probably not. Animals in the wild simply don't get fat. Survival is a full-time job for a wild animal, a nonstop struggle that burns calories and shapes the course of his entire life. A wild animal hunts, runs, plays, and performs all manner of strenuous activities each day, all the while contending with extremes in temperature and environment. There is almost no chance that one of these magnificent survivors could ever become overweight. And if one ever managed to actually do so, he wouldn't be able to hunt effectively, or even protect himself against other predators. Obesity, in other words, would be his death sentence.

Not so with the domestic dog or cat. Blessed with loving owners, a safe, warm household, and plenty of food, America's favorite pets have precious few concerns compared to their wild cousins. Because of domesticity's less harried pace and greatly reduced territorial range, our pets burn far fewer calories on a daily basis than do wolves, coyotes, lions, or cheetahs. While the lean leader of a wolf pack in the wilds of

Alaska is fast on the heels of a mule deer, your Labrador retriever is fast asleep in front of a cozy fireplace. As a cheetah rockets across the African savannah at nearly seventy miles per hour in hungry pursuit of an elusive impala, your pampered tabby lazily lounges on your cushy king-sized bed.

Obesity, clinically defined as being 15 percent or more over the target weight, is the most common nutritional disorder among dogs and cats. *Over 25 percent of all domestic canines and felines in this country are significantly overweight.* These millions of beloved pets will live shorter lives and be prone to a host of disorders and diseases ranging from hip, back, shoulder, knee, and foot problems to hypertension, stroke, increased risk of cancer, diabetes, liver and kidney dysfunction, heat exhaustion, respiratory difficulties, and heart disease—to name but a few. It is sad but true that a cat or dog who remains obese for more than a few years will have a contracted, uncomfortable existence.

Like a human, a dog or cat becomes overweight when her intake of calories exceeds her body's energy expenditures, and the mounting surplus of calories is stored as fat. As both cats and dogs are on average much smaller than humans, pet obesity can result even with a daily excess of only a small percentage—or a few ounces of food. Within a year or two, your German shepherd or Siamese could become morbidly obese.

How to Tell If Your Pet Is Overweight

For many owners, determining if their dog or cat is overweight is not an easy task, for a number of reasons. Many breeds of dogs and cats have medium to long coats, which can hide the early signs of weight gain. Pets with relatively short coats, however, will not be able to hide much more than a 5 percent weight increase from a reasonably observant owner. Smaller pets will in general show weight gains faster than larger ones, making it easier for the owners of cats and small dogs to detect increases. The owners of inherently thin breeds (such as whippets or Cornish rexes) will be more quickly aware of their pets' weight gain than will owners of heftier breeds, such as Rottweilers or Persians. These variations aside, the common signs of obesity in a dog or cat include:

- *An overall thick appearance,* particularly in the waist, which in a fit animal would taper nicely from the chest to the loins (much more so in the dog than in the cat). The overweight dog or cat's head and legs will appear smaller than normal.

- *A palpable layer of fat over the ribs and stomach,* obscuring any signs of the rib cage. A fit cat should have only a thin layer of fat between the skin and the musculature covering the rib cage; his ribs should be easy to feel with your fingertips. With a dog, the lines of the rib cage should be just barely visible. The fat on an obese dog or cat's chest will completely obscure the shape of the rib cage.

- *The stomach of an obese dog or cat will hang down,* often to the same level as the upper rib cage, giving the pet's body a rectangular shape.

- *The pet will have a slower, more deliberate, almost plodding gait,* resulting from the skeletal structure having to support weight it was not designed for. The obese cat or dog will often take smaller steps, and will rarely be as active or agile as an animal of normal proportions. The obese cat will not be as capable of jumping vertically or leaping horizontally. The obese dog will not be able to jump over objects such as fences or hedges and could easily injure herself in trying.

- *Increased lethargy and sleep time.* The obese dog or cat will tire more quickly and will have a higher respiratory and heart rate than that of a fit pet. Overheating (as evidenced by panting, drooling, and increased water intake) is common among overweight cats and dogs.

- *Hair and skin problems* ranging from a greasy, sparse, or dry coat to dandruff, rashes, or sores. The obese cat may not be able to groom himself adequately, resulting in a disheveled appearance and an unpleasant odor.

- *Constipation, diarrhea, or house-training setbacks.*

- *Moody or irritable behavior* caused in part by the pet's physical discomfort.

- *Obsessive-compulsive behaviors,* particularly with regard to eating, begging, and incessant vocalizations.

- *An increased aggression* toward animals, people, or both, particularly relating to food guarding or territoriality.

- *An increased incidence of tooth decay* caused by more time spent eating.

- *A higher incidence of injury,* particularly muscle, tendon, or ligament damage. Back, hip, shoulder, knee, or foot problems are likely, due to the increased stress on these parts.

- *Poor overall health,* caused by a greater strain on the immune, digestive, respiratory, and cardiovascular systems.

Of course, the majority of owners can tell if their pets are overweight (even if they won't readily admit it) simply by observing their companions on a day-to-day basis. Those in the practice of weighing their dogs or cats will be able to tell for sure, though few actually get around to doing so, particularly when dealing with a large breed of dog. Infrequent visitors to the home will often be the first to pick up on a pet's weight increase due to the elapsed time between visits. Most friends or guests choose not to say anything, however, for fear of offending their hosts.

If you have doubts about whether your pet is overweight, the simplest, surest solution is to schedule a visit with your veterinarian, who will quickly determine if your dog or cat is carrying excess pounds. This visit is crucial, not only to identify your pet's weight status, but also to determine if her overall health has been permanently affected. In addition, the veterinarian will be able to tell if the obesity is being caused by a medical problem, such as a hormonal imbalance. Through weighing, observation, and handling, your vet will easily be able to give you an impartial, definitive answer to the question, "Is my pet fat?"

Causes of Obesity

As stated earlier, any dog or cat who takes in more calories than he burns up will gain weight. Sounds simple, doesn't it? Unfortunately for your pet, it is not so cut-and-dry. Although the bottom line is *caloric intake versus caloric expenditure*, there are factors in a pet's life that affect these two quantities, and these factors ultimately will directly influence your companion's weight. Obviously, caloric intake is determined solely by what (and how much) your dog or cat eats each day. The combined calories consumed from meals, treats, handouts, or captured animals (in the case of some predatory outdoor cats) must be considered in order to be completely accurate. Caloric expenditure is determined by the pet's metabolism and by how active she is. An old sedentary Clumber spaniel, for instance, will burn many fewer calories in a day than will a six-month-old pointer puppy. Though the factors that affect caloric expenditure far outnumber those that determine intake, careful monitoring of both is the only way to reduce an obese pet's weight.

The following section details the factors that can contribute to obesity in dogs and cats. Understanding the implications of each will help you formulate a plan that successfully allows your pet to lose weight and gain health.

Nature versus Domesticity

For eons animals in the wild have had natural controls that determine their weight and metabolism. Being predators, wild felines and canines must search out, hunt down, and capture their meals, a task dependent on the range and availability of prey animals, climate, terrain, time of year, and many other variables. They have to work hard to find a meal, unlike Fido and Sylvester, who need only lumber into the kitchen and stick their noses into heaping bowls of kibble. Often, wolves, wild dogs, lions, or leopards will go for days without satisfying their hunger drives.

Wild animals must also compete with other predators for nature's sometimes elusive bounty. A wolf pack consisting of seven or eight members might track down and kill an elk, only to discover that they have accidentally entered the territory of a larger rival pack. Though hungry and excited from the kill, they are outnumbered and must retreat. Similarly, a leopard might kill an antelope, only to be chased off by a much larger tiger. These instances result in missed meals, despite great expenditures of energy.

Mating and reproductive efforts also tend to use up great amounts of energy in the wild. Finding and winning over a mate can be strenuous, difficult, and even dangerous, particularly when other animals are competing for the same mate. Pregnancy, birthing, and the rearing of young also use up tremendous stores of energy, and they make regular hunting and feeding all the more difficult, which sometimes results in weight loss.

Domestic cats and dogs have little or no worries over competition with other animals for food or mates, because owners provide for everything. With regard to reproduction, most owners either neuter their pets, or, in the case of purebred show animals, follow carefully choreographed breeding procedures free from any dangers or competition.

Wild felines or canines who become underweight or overweight usually do not survive for very long. A sickly, underweight animal becomes too weak to hunt and eventually falls victim to some other predator. An overweight animal (almost nonexistent in the wild) would be too slow and clumsy and would quickly succumb to more capable creatures. Only the fittest, strongest examples of the species survive and reproduce. Nature and her demands, though harsh, see to it that weight disorders have no place in the wild.

The taming of dogs and cats has succeeded in removing all of these natural controls. Our pets, unlike their wild cousins, can depend on obtaining a steady source of food without undergoing much competitive stress. Whereas a wolf or cheetah might travel upward of thirty to forty miles to find a meal, most domestic cats or dogs need only walk thirty to forty feet to do the same. The decreased physical demands of domesticity have therefore turned down our pets' internal metabolic "thermostats," lowering the number of calories they need to maintain ideal body weight.

Curiously, what has not significantly decreased over the years is the domestic dog or cat's prey or "food" drive. Your basic tabby and terrier still maintain most of their ancestral instincts to hunt down and eat prey. In fact, most domestic dogs or cats would eat four or five times the amount of food normally offered to them if given the chance, a throwback to the ingrained habit of most wild predators to gorge on a kill because the next kill might be days or even weeks away. The retention of this ancient drive, in combination with the domestic pet's reduced caloric expenditure and slower metabolism, creates the dilemma: Domestic cats and dogs want to eat as much as their wild cousins, but they cannot without becoming obese.

Another factor that helps keep wild felines and canines from becoming overweight is their higher incidence, compared to domestic animals, of illness, injury, infection, and premature death. A pet suffering from a bad respiratory infection or a severe laceration can be brought to a local veterinary clinic for prompt and effective treatment, and he will recover nicely in most cases. But a cheetah or hyena suffering from similar problems could easily die. In other words, wild dogs and cats have a much higher incidence of early mortality. An animal who lives a shorter, more injury- or disease-prone life will have little chance of becoming obese.

In comparison, your favorite dog or cat gets top-notch treatment. On-call veterinary clinics, a steady supply of nutritious food, a secure, warm, safe environment, and a protective owner all help to lower mortality rates and lengthen life spans, giving your pet the opportunity to become overweight. As stated earlier, only under conditions of security and abundance can obesity exist at all.

Poor Owner Awareness of Proper Pet Nutrition

Let's face it: Your pet doesn't get up in the morning and fix herself a cup of coffee, two fried eggs, four strips of bacon, and two slices of buttered toast. It is your hand that meters out all food, treats, and table scraps. Taking full responsibility for feeding our pets is one of the chores of domesticity we have agreed to in exchange for the companionship we seek.

Unfortunately, many owners know little about proper pet nutrition, and even less about how much to feed their particular pet. Correct feeding technique can also be a mystery to many: Some feed too often, others not often enough. Some provide food on a continuous basis. Others overdo treats and table scraps, another mistake that can lead to obesity. Let's examine the most common feeding errors individually so you can understand just how each may contribute to the problem.

Feeding the wrong type of food to a pet may result in obesity, simply because the food in question contains more calories per normal serving than the pet needs to maintain ideal body weight. For example, many owners, after finding a quality commercial dog or cat food that their pet likes, stick with that food throughout the pet's adult years and into old age. This practice, unfortunately, is one of the most common causes of obesity in pets. A food that provides a pet with three hundred calories per cup, for instance, might work just fine for a three-year-old dog, but it could have too many calories for the same pet when he reaches eight to nine years of age. The owner of this dog, used to the routine of buying the same food each month (and appreciative of his or her pet actually liking the taste of the brand), continues serving it in the same quantities to the older animal, whose slowing metabolism no longer needs so many calories. Though eating the same quantity as always, the dog slowly becomes obese.

Other owners simply feed their dogs or cats too darn much. Rather than checking the pet food label for proper feeding guidelines (or discussing it with a veterinarian), some pet owners simply guess at the right amount. Dry foods especially can be overfed to cats and dogs, as they tend to be more highly concentrated sources of calories than canned, semimoist, or home-cooked diets. Give a cat or dog twice the necessary amount of food at each meal and you will be sure to end up with a plump pup or fat cat within the month.

Some owners do manage to feed the proper amounts of food to their pets, only to forget about treats and table scraps liberally offered throughout the day. Leftover bits of meat or cheese are especially high in fat and can provide hundreds of surplus calories. Many owners are shocked to learn that the treats they routinely give their dogs and cats contain more calories than the pets' actual feedings!

Another very common feeding error made by owners (especially of cats or toy dogs) is the practice of free-feeding, or providing a steady supply of food to the pet all day long. Many well-meaning owners, gone at work all day, will leave a large bowl of dry food down on the floor for their cats or dogs to enjoy whenever they choose, thinking this will in some way occupy the pets' time, or be a comfort while left alone. Owners who always keep food in a bowl routinely replenish the supply whenever it runs low. This practice can cause obesity in a number of ways: First, when a cat or dog has a constant supply of food available, she will quickly reach a state in which she is not ever really hungry, but instead always nearly satiated. This pet will end up picking at her food all day. Though eating less at each feeding, the pet ends up eating more than if the owner had fed her one or two twenty-minute meals. The lesson learned here is that all-day "snacking" leads to obesity. Cats or dogs with above-average food drives will suffer the most from this type of feeding because they will constantly empty their bowls—and their owners will constantly refill them. These pets will end up eating two to three times the amount of food necessary to maintain ideal body weight, turning into ponderous, obsessive eating machines.

A second negative aspect of free-feeding a dog or cat is that it causes the digestive process to work full-steam throughout the day. This causes the pet to become sleepy and lethargic, discouraging any calorie-burning activity. Any pet who is constantly lying around digesting will have a slower metabolism, resulting in lower caloric expenditures.

The practice of free-feeding does not even benefit a finicky, underweight pet. In supplying a constant source of food to encourage a thin cat or dog to put on weight, owners of these pets actually accomplish the opposite. Think about it: What conditions must occur in the wild for a wolf or tiger to become famished? Certainly not abundance. If prey were plentiful and easily procured, these predators would eat their fill and quickly become satiated, and, consequently, their food drive would diminish. Animal trainers who work with large predators know that if they want to reduce the chances of an attack, they must simply make sure the animal has been well fed before being handled. The same holds true for your cat or dog: Providing a finicky pet with a constant supply of food will actually lower his food drive, further compounding the problem. So, free-feeding your dog or cat fails on both ends of the weight spectrum: It fattens up pets with normal or high food drives, and it makes finicky eaters even more selective.

Lack of Activity

Today's dogs and cats lead much more sedentary lives than pets of the past. It used to be that Fido and Sylvester could spend large parts of their days outside chasing squirrels or Frisbees, or simply romping through country fields, with little chance of encountering danger. Most of you can recall a time when a pet from your past was able to run, jump, climb trees, or swim in a creek, all in the name of good fun. Other pets served more utilitarian outdoor roles, working as herders, ratters, guardians, or hunters. In the process, these pets burned lots of calories and were in peak physical condition.

Unfortunately, pets these days cannot be afforded this level of outdoor freedom, for a number of reasons. The majority of today's human population resides in busy urban or suburban environments, making any kind of unsupervised, independent pet activity virtually impossible. Any dog or cat roaming on her own on West Eighty-sixth Street in Upper Manhattan would have a projected life span of about three minutes, if that. The dangers posed by cars, trucks, and buses, combined with all the other dangers and stresses of outdoor urban life, would simply be too much for most pets. Because of this, pets today (even in the burgeoning suburbs) are kept indoors much of the time. When they are taken outside, it is usually under close supervision and controlled conditions. In my opinion, this is prudent, as any pet allowed to roam freely could be killed or infected with any number of deadly canine or feline viruses circulating among stray, diseased, and wild animals. Indoor/outdoor cats are especially susceptible to diseases such as rabies, feline panleukopenia, feline calicivirus, feline immunodeficiency virus, and a host of other deadly contagions passed during casual contact with other cats or with feces. Most owners who allow their cats unrestricted access to the outdoors do not consider these dangers, or the consequence of their cats reproducing and contributing to the terrible problem we have with unwanted cats. Dogs, being somewhat less able to cope on their own in busy residential areas, should never be let out on their own.

The need to keep dogs and cats indoors much of the time causes them to burn far fewer calories on a daily basis than did pets of the past, contributing to a gradual but steady increase in the average pet's weight. Many pets left alone at home by busy working owners develop a sedentary lifestyle and passive mind-set, setting the stage for obesity. These "latchkey" pets sleep away most of the day, half-heartedly nibble at food, and end up so incredibly bored from a total lack of stimulation and companionship that they often develop physiological or psychological problems, including destructive behavior, obsessive-compulsive behavior, excessive vocalizations, skin disorders, hair loss, or extreme antisocial tendencies. These pets lose much of their muscle mass, which slows down their metabolic rates and further reduces their ability to maintain ideal weight. Barely active, soft muscled, and isolated, these dogs and cats have little to prevent weight gain.

Even when an owner is present, rarely is an effort made to relieve his or her pet's boredom. Most greet the pet upon returning home, play with him for a few minutes, and (in the case of a dog) perhaps take him out for a walk. Then the owner goes about his or her business, leaving the pet to amuse himself again, as he had to during the day. Though the presence of the owner is a comfort, it is not a remedy for boredom, a key factor in dog and cat obesity. Most owners put their routines at home over their pets' needs, not stopping to think that their dogs and cats are being neglected. These pets often do not seem neglected, except for their dull behavior and weight gain.

As stated earlier, domestic dogs and cats live in a dramatically smaller world than do their wild cousins. This reduced territorial range translates to less activity, meaning fewer calories burned. In addition, your pet's territory, though reduced in size, is much more secure from other competitors, virtually eliminating territorial and sexual competition with other animals. Overall, there is much less social and emotional activity, contributing to further metabolic slowdown. When a pack of wolves defends its territory from a rival pack, each member of the squad experiences a heightened state of readiness and a resulting increase in calories burned. Likewise, when a male leopard courts a female in heat, his level of sexual tension (combined with the potential of combat with other male competitors) raises the metabolic bar yet again. Most pets, removed from territorial or sexual competition, never experience that metabolic boost. Their sense of security leads to a more laid-back, cloistered mind-set. Though a safe environment is beneficial to a pet's psyche and overall physical health, the resulting reduction in activity in comparison to wild predators means a higher risk of obesity.

Lack of Socialization

In the wild, canines, such as wolves, are among the most sociable creatures on the planet. From birth they interact with their fellow pack members in very sophisticated ways, building a complex hierarchical structure that helps define the species. Isolated from others of its kind, the wolf would become stressed and ineffectual and in all likelihood would find hunting and feeding nearly impossible, given that wolves depend on teamwork to bring down prey that is often larger than themselves.

Wild cats (with the exception of lions and cheetahs) are more isolated in the wild and do not crave or rely on companionship as keenly as wild canines. These felines do, however, come together to mate at least once per year; females also spend at least one full year raising offspring, who enjoy the companionship of their littermates until they are forced by their mothers to go out on their own. Juvenile felines, denied the company of their littermates during the first year of life, would suffer developmentally and show great fear of other cats. None would be able to mate later in life due to their profound antisocial tendencies. The isolation of cats at an early age might therefore lead to the extinction of the species.

Clearly, both wild canines and felines need some level of socialization to develop normally. This applies to the domestic dog or cat as well. With no opportunity to regularly interact with other animals or humans outside of the family, these pets can become antisocial, overly territorial, and stressed, all behavioral abnormalities that can actually increase the food drive (as evidenced by nervous or displacement eating, common among isolated humans). Just as we often turn to food for solace and comfort, so too can troubled and lonely dogs and cats.

Though more vital in dogs, companionship for cats is also necessary. Most pet cats view owners as either substitute parents or siblings, due to domesticity's ability to extend the feline "childhood" indefinitely. These perpetual juveniles never quite break out of the litter mentality, which in the wild still allows a high level of socializing. So, your adult domestic cat behaves in a much more "childlike" manner than does any wild feline and will crave a good amount of companionship, at least with humans.

Today's pet spends much of her days alone, twiddling her paws, so to speak. This can result in overeating, a symptom of isolation. Common in humans cut off from intimate contact with others, obsessive-compulsive eating in dogs and cats is a sure road to obesity and poor health.

Poor Owner Control

Let's face it: A poorly behaved dog or cat is a pain. Nothing can cloud your day faster than a dog who doesn't come when called, or a cat who marks on or rips up the sofa. Unfortunately, many pets do develop troublesome behaviors, causing the majority of owners grief and confusion. What's an owner to do?

Due to a lack of leadership and supervisory skills, owners often set themselves up for trouble with their pets, who have the same basic reasoning capacity of a two-year-old human child. Those of you who are parents know that two-year-olds can get into as much trouble as you'll let them. Pet owners who allow bad behaviors to develop in their four-legged friends often fall into the trap of continually bribing their little tyrants with fattening treats, in an attempt to obtain some sort of short-lived, ineffective obedience. These "caloric distractions" not only serve to merely briefly halt an undesirable behavior, but also tend to reinforce the unwanted acts. Think about it: If I gave you ten dollars every time you tossed a piece of litter out your car window, would you soon give up the behavior? Hardly. The same mind-set develops with your pet. Give a dog a treat to get him off the sofa and he will continue jumping up there to keep the snacks coming. Frustrated owners not able to permanently stop bad behaviors in their pets resort to food bribery. If this habit becomes ingrained, the dog or cat becomes fat.

Metabolic Abnormalities

A small percentage of dogs and cats can become obese despite having a proper diet and getting plenty of exercise. The cause of this is sometimes an imbalance or dysfunction of the endocrine system. Normally responsible for mediating myriad bodily functions through the production and secretion of hormones, this important system regulates metabolism, sexual development and function, stress response, temperature regulation, growth, and a host of other operations. Basically a chemical messenger service, your pet's endocrine system turns messages from the brain into actual metabolic processes. The glands of the endocrine system release their hormones directly into the bloodstream, which then carries them to the appropriate areas in the body. Hormones mediate every possible aspect of a dog or cat's physiology, from breathing and heartbeat to reproduction and bone growth, and even attitude and appetite changes. The glands in your pet's endocrine system include:

- adrenal glands
- hypothalamus
- pituitary gland
- pancreas
- parathyroid glands
- testes (in males)
- ovaries (in females)
- thyroid gland

The endocrine gland that has the most profound effects on a dog or cat's weight is the thyroid gland, which acts as the body's thermostat, controlling your pet's level of metabolic activity. A thyroid gland producing too little thyroid hormone (a condition called *hypothyroidism*) will cause an animal's metabolism to slow down dramatically; this in turn reduces calories burned by normal body functions. A dog or cat suffering from this disorder can become obese, even when eating what would normally be the correct number of calories. The opposite problem, known as *hyperthyroidism*, acts in the reverse, turning up the metabolic thermostat and causing weight loss, even when the pet eats more than necessary to maintain weight.

Enteroendocrine cells in your pet's digestive tract secrete a number of hormones important to digestion as well as to regulation of the appetite. If the process of secretion goes awry, your cat or dog could experience a change in digestive patterns or hunger drive, possibly resulting in obesity.

The *pancreas* is known for its role in secreting *insulin*, the hormone that regulates blood sugar levels as well as fat and protein metabolism. What is less known is that insulin levels also affect your dog or cat's appetite through stimulation of the *hypothalamus*, another important gland located in the brain. Incorrect levels of insulin in your pet's body can increase a pet's appetite, causing obesity.

A dysfunctional endocrine system in a dog or cat is uncommon and normally will not be the reason why your pet is obese. Your veterinarian, however, will want to run blood, urine, and fecal tests just to eliminate the chance that your overweight pet might in fact have hormonal imbalances. This is a key reason why you should bring your overweight pet into the veterinarian. Prompt action on your part could solve the weight problem, and even save your pet's life.

Neutering

Though sterilization of a dog or cat through surgical means is generally referred to as neutering, the more accurate terminology is *castration* for the male and *spay* for the female. Castration involves the removal of the male pet's testes; spaying involves removal of the female's uterus and ovaries. In either case, the pet in question is permanently prevented from breeding.

The benefits of neutering your pet far outweigh the disadvantages. In addition to preventing unwanted puppies and kittens, the procedure dramatically reduces incidences of aggression, marking behavior, and destruction of property, and it minimizes the desire in both sexes to roam. Overall behavior is improved, and obedience training is easier to implement.

A neutered cat or dog will experience a very slight slowdown in metabolism, requiring owners to reduce the amount of food served by a small percentage, or to increase exercise by the same amount. The effects of this are almost negligible; most owners won't even notice a change. Unfortunately, some owners like to blame neutering for their pet's obesity. Nothing could be more incorrect: If a pet is fat, his owners are feeding him too much and exercising him too little. To repeat: Neutering is not to blame.

Effects of Obesity

All aspects of your pet's health will be adversely affected by being 15 percent or more over ideal weight. Her physical and psychological well-being will suffer, as will her ability to interact and play with you and your family. A fat dog or cat simply won't have as much fun as will a trimmer, fitter pet. In addition, the cost to you of maintaining such a pet will be higher, both financially and emotionally. More frequent trips to the veterinarian will be likely, as an obese pet's health often suffers tremendously. Given that even a preventive trip to the veterinarian can cost over fifty dollars, frequent visits can really add up. Statistically, obese cats and dogs also live shorter lives than do fit pets. The sight of your companion suffering and not being able to function properly will weigh on you, causing emotional stress and guilt that could actually affect *your* health.

Physiological Effects

Carrying excess weight for extended periods will open your pet up to numerous life-threatening disorders. The extra pounds can, over time, cause increased wear and tear on the pet's joints, ligaments, and tendons, eventually causing pain that requires veterinary attention, and perhaps even surgery. Though more common in medium to large dogs than in cats, either species can suffer structural injuries to the feet, knees, hips, back, or shoulders if carrying too much weight for too long. The pet who is used to being active runs an even greater risk of this and will suffer more muscle pulls, strains, and tears, as he tries to be as spry and active as he was during slimmer times. Firmly ingrained behavior patterns are hard to change: The dog who while slim looked forward to fetching a Frisbee every day will try to continue this behavior even when obese, possibly resulting in injury. The cat used to leaping down to the carpet from atop a tall dresser will try to continue that behavior even after becoming obese, possibly resulting in muscle damage, stress fractures, or worse. It's analogous to you strapping on a thirty- or forty-pound backpack and playing full-court basketball for an hour. Odds are you will hurt yourself; the spirit's willing, but the body isn't up to the task. If not addressed, the constant strain on your pet's overloaded body could lead to permanent damage.

A more serious side effect of pet obesity is the added strain it puts on the heart and lungs. Designed to operate in a body of a certain weight, a heart forced to function in a substantially heavier body will strain to do its job, much like the engine of an overloaded car trying to get up a steep hill. Over time this can cause heart disease and a shortened life span. The lungs of an overweight pet will also be working overtime to provide the oxygen needed to keep the laboring heart and muscles working. An overweight dog or cat will generally be aerobically unfit, resulting in rapid exhaustion, excessive panting, and possible dehydration.

Liver and kidney disease is more prevalent in the obese pet. As obesity often results from too fatty a diet, these important filtering and purifying organs will work overtime in an attempt to metabolize the richer diet. This can cause reduced function or disease.

A fatty diet can also result in more cancers, particularly of the digestive tract, liver, or skin. Even strokes are more likely to occur in an obese pet than in a trim, healthy one (although they're much less common in dogs and cats than in humans).

An obese pet's immune system will be forced to work harder due to the strain put on all the body systems, often resulting in more frequent and protracted illnesses and infections. If taxed, the immune system could also malfunction and turn against the body, causing autoimmune problems and allergic reactions, such as intestinal damage, fatigue, and chronic viral infections.

Statistically, the fatter a pet becomes, the greater her chance of developing *diabetes mellitus*, a disease of the pancreas that causes a decrease in the production of *insulin*. Because insulin makes it possible for glucose in the blood to enter the body's cells and be used as fuel, without enough the sugar remains in the blood and is eventually passed out of the body in the urine. If not treated, diabetes can be fatal. Ironically, the latter stages of diabetes result in slow, steady weight loss, due to little fuel getting into the cells, which begin to starve and die. Obesity seems to adversely affect the function of the pancreas, leading to the condition.

Behavioral Effects

Being chronically obese can cause all manner of undesirable pet behaviors. An overweight pet will not be happy due to the extra pounds, which restrict movement, create stress and strain on all the body parts, and worsen overall health. An unhappy dog or cat is very likely to express unhappiness in a number of undesirable (and inappropriate) ways, including:

HOUSE-TRAINING MISHAPS

The obese pet is much more likely to have accidents around the home, or to purposely defecate or urinate in an inappropriate place, as a way of releasing anxiety. Also, a pet being fed lots of fatty table scraps could end up developing diarrhea because cats' and dogs' digestive tracts are not adept at dealing with varying types of human food. The obese pet might also vomit up indigestible offerings.

DESTRUCTIVE BEHAVIOR

An unhappy obese pet might also express her feelings by becoming a destructive little nuisance, chewing up shoes, television or VCR remote control devices, wires, carpets, clothing, or any manner of valuable items not yet meant for the scrap heap. Furniture can often be scratched or ripped apart, garbage pails raided, pants eaten (or eliminated on), and curtains destroyed. Outdoors, pets can destroy gardens, lawns, or fences, or dig holes all over the yard. Remember that an unhappy pet with no way to express her anxiety will find some concrete way to release her frustrations, usually to the detriment of your wallet.

OUTRIGHT DISOBEDIENCE

The obese pet, suffering anxiety due to his condition, will often ignore you when asked to do something (or not do something). In addition to being frustrated by his condition, an obese dog or cat will most likely have an obsessive-compulsive desire to eat, a desire so strong that all other influences (including you) will most likely take a backseat. Eating, though the cause of his problems, becomes the most important activity in the pet's life, making it a powerful motivator and master. If given the choice between crossing the street to eat pet food left out on the deck by a neighbor and obeying your "come" command, most fat pets will obey their stomachs and not you.

AGGRESSION

An obese dog or cat whose life centers around eating will be much more likely to show aggression toward other animals or toward humans, due to her coveting of food. Food guarding, a prime cause of aggression in dogs and cats, becomes much more likely with the obese pet, whose favorite spot in the home is two inches above her food bowl. For example, if a toddler happens to wander up close to an obese dog or cat's food bowl while the pet is present, chances are the pet will become territorial, resulting in a growl, hiss, scratch, or bite. A trim pet who does not fixate on food would be less likely to have this type of inappropriate reaction.

EXCESSIVE SLEEPING

An overweight pet, having more food in his digestive tract at any given time, will be more sluggish and sleepy than would a healthy pet, resulting in increased sleep time, fewer calories burned in a day, and an increased likelihood of even greater obesity.

ANTISOCIAL BEHAVIOR

An obese pet will most likely be kept at home more often than would a healthy, active animal, simply because she won't be capable of running and playing as much. The same is true of obese humans, who sadly shy away from outdoor activities such as soccer, softball, Frisbee, or hiking because they can't physically participate as competently. After years of being kept home, obese pets can become very territorial and suspicious of strangers, resulting in a loss of desire to interact with other pets or persons outside of the immediate family. This behavior prevents the obese pet from properly socializing, which in turn eliminates the exercise she might get from playing and interacting.

As you can see, the causes of obesity in dogs and cats are varied, and the effects serious. If you were to ask your veterinarian what situations most threaten the health of dogs and cats today, he or she would most likely list cars, viral infections, and obesity as the top three killers. Not as much can be done by you with regard to the first two threats, save for training your dog well, moving to a less populated area, and getting your pet properly vaccinated. Luckily, much can be done by you to eliminate the third killer from your pet's life. Pet obesity is for the most part an owner-induced disease and can be easily prevented, provided you follow certain guidelines with respect to how you feed your pet, and how you manage his lifestyle.

The following chapters are designed to provide you with a comprehensive plan of action that will trim down and perk up your portly pal and give her a much happier and more stimulating lifestyle. Just think about how much happier *you* would be if you lost 15 or 20 percent of your body weight in excess fat (which in the average human would be equal to about twenty to forty pounds). You would feel livelier, healthier, and much more confident in your appearance and physical capabilities. Your dog or cat, freed of her fatty burden, will enjoy the same benefits, and she will be extremely grateful to you for your love and concern.

1. Identify the Cause and Extent of Your Pet's Obesity

As you have read in the introduction, a pet's overweight condition can be caused by one of a number of factors, or by a combination of several. Before you can begin to help your dog or cat, you therefore will first need to identify just how overweight your pet is, and what factors are causing the obesity.

Some of you will know the answers to these key questions, whereas others might not be so sure. In either case, I strongly recommend you incorporate the following two steps into your pet's weight loss plan, as they are designed to make clear to you exactly how overweight your dog or cat is, how much his health has been compromised, how much food he is eating each day, and just what his level of daily activity is. By clearly defining the problem and its causes, you will be able to initiate a plan of action that will help your pet get back to good health. The love you have for your companion demands nothing less.

Schedule a Visit with a Veterinarian

Next to you, the most important person in your pet's life is the veterinarian. A competent vet does much more than just tend to injuries or administer vaccinations. He or she, under ideal conditions, becomes your pet's friend and guardian, looking out for signs of approaching illness, helping prevent disorders before they occur, and giving sound advice in many areas, from behavioral problems and diet recommendations to birthing, pet transport, and much more.

Unfortunately, many owners do not bring their dogs or cats into the veterinarian on a regular basis, but instead wait until some emergency arises. Others visit the veterinarian simply to get yearly inoculations, or for help with parasitic infestations. Denied the regular attention of a caring health professional, your pet could easily develop a disease or disorder that would put her life in jeopardy.

The first step in reducing your dog or cat's weight is to schedule a visit with a skilled veterinarian who, after first assessing the animal's overall health, will determine if your pet is overweight, and if so, by how much. An experienced veterinarian will be knowledgeable about a particular pet's optimal weight, which is based on breed, frame, gender, and age. He or she will weigh your pet and give you an idea of the animal's target weight. When given this information, many owners become shocked, embarrassed, or angry. Some even go into denial, feeling that their vet couldn't possibly be serious about Sylvester or Fido being five, ten, or even twenty pounds overweight. Don't let this happen to you: Trust that your veterinarian knows what the truth is, and accept that your companion needs to shed some pounds. It doesn't mean you are a bad owner; it just means you need to learn more about your pet's metabolism and lifestyle.

During this visit, your veterinarian will determine if there are any medical causes for the obesity (such as a hormonal imbalance). In addition, blood, urine, and stool samples will be examined to determine if any corollary disorders exist, such as diabetes or heart or liver disease. The veterinarian will listen closely to your pet's heart and lungs to see whether they have been damaged or overworked. Your pet's musculoskeletal system will be examined in an attempt to determine if the extra weight has begun to cause arthritic problems; joint, ligament, or tendon strains; or muscle pulls or strains. The pet's gait will be examined, as will his coat, skin, teeth, and overall hygiene, often the first areas to show the debilitating effects of obesity. For example, an obese cat may not be able to reach around to clean his anal area, resulting in bad odor, matted hair, and dried fecal matter clinging to the cat's coat.

In addition to determining your dog or cat's overall health, your vet will be able to give you valuable advice on diet, particularly what types of food might be best suited to your pet's metabolism. Equally important will be your veterinarian's opinion on what level of activity your pet will be able to participate in, based on how overweight she is. For example, a fifty-pound beagle (nearly twice the breed's ideal weight) could seriously damage herself if suddenly required to jog two miles a day with a well-meaning but uninformed owner. A good veterinarian will be able to help you design and implement a prudent exercise regimen for your pet, one that won't do more harm than good.

Choosing a qualified veterinarian for your pet is important and should be done with care. First consider location, as well as hours of operation. Ideally, you should locate a veterinary clinic that is within ten or fifteen minutes of your residence, so that your dog or cat needn't endure a long car ride if sick or injured; a long car ride could be fatal to a seriously injured animal. Also, make sure the clinic's hours are convenient for you. Check to see that they have at least one or two days during the week with evening hours, allowing you to take your pet for a checkup after work.

Emergencies never happen when you want them to, so choose a veterinarian who is able to provide efficient emergency care to his or her clients, or who can at least refer you to a nearby emergency after-hours clinic when needed. This convenience could one day save your pet's life.

A veterinarian should be reasonably priced. Though this shouldn't be your only criterion, price nevertheless factors into the decision-making process. Also, avoid high-volume clinics whose prices are substantially below those of other clinics in the area.

The veterinarian's office should be organized and well run. The presence of irate clients, dog or cat fights, or sick pets waiting endlessly in the reception area (possibly infecting others) should be a red flag to you to leave. The staff should be polite and efficient, and your appointment time should be honored (within reason). In addition, the clinic should appear clean, with no disagreeable smells or messes evident.

Choose a veterinarian who seems easy to communicate with, and who likes to listen. A vet should have good people skills and be able to explain things clearly, without too much technical jargon. If you do not feel comfortable with a veterinarian, by all means find another with whom you are more at ease.

Select a veterinarian who allows you to be present during your dog or cat's exam (though do not expect to be present for surgeries or emergency care). You can learn a lot about your pet by closely observing veterinary procedures.

A good method for choosing a vet is asking friends or family for a recommendation. If they have been with the same professional for years, chances are the vet will satisfy you as well.

The shelter or breeder from which you obtained your pet can probably recommend a qualified vet in your area. They deal with dozens of animals on a daily basis and depend on quality medical care. Their vet just might be the one for you.

If all else fails, check the yellow pages. Though you won't know anything about the clinics listed, you can check out a few and see if you feel comfortable with each. Normally, veterinarians are a caring, informed group; you should be able to find someone quickly. Just make sure you feel at ease with the doctor and his or her staff.

The Control Week

Many weight loss plans for humans incorporate a technique designed to show participants just how much food they are eating each day, as well as how much exercise they are actually getting. For a set period (often a day or a week), they are required to keep a detailed log of everything they eat and what activities they participate in. After recording every morsel of food, many participants are shocked to find that their intake is substantially higher than they ever imagined it was. Snacks, alcoholic beverages, cups of coffee (with lots of cream and sugar), and other between-meal treats add hundreds of calories to the daily intake. Meals also end up being much more caloric than first thought, particularly with respect to the size of the portions served, and the number of calories derived from fat.

Many are also shocked to discover that much of the activity they do each day, consisting mostly of walking or some minor lifting, is only minimally strenuous. Even those who go to a gym on a regular basis find that the half hour they spend on the treadmill burns about the same number of calories in the small bag of potato chips they had at lunch. Though sometimes initially discouraging, the technique of recording everything eaten and everything done during a set period can be one of the more effective dieting tools.

Why not utilize this same technique with your over-weight dog or cat? Most owners have absolutely no idea just how much their pets are actually eating each day, often erroneously thinking that the bulk of calories are contained in the scheduled feedings. In fact, most overweight pets have gained their weight more from the snacks between meals than from meals themselves. This is often a source of confusion for owners, who ask, "I'm only feeding her one little cup of food for dinner; how could she get fat on that?" The answer often lies in all the treats given throughout the day by various family members, each one not knowing what the others are doing.

Also, owners tend to think of all dogs or cats as being naturally active, and therefore not as in need of exercise as humans. This is nonsense. As stated earlier, pets today are nowhere near as active as those of years ago, and are probably even less active than their owners, who, in an effort to stay fit and healthy, diligently schedule workouts at the gym, jog, or participate in sports or some other aerobic activity. Recording your pet's activity levels for a set period will reveal just how sedentary his life is.

Of course, your dog or cat probably cannot write, so you will have to take control of this project. To that end, you will need to keep a *detailed, week-long record* of exactly what (and when) your pet eats, as well as a record of everything she does, such as eat, sleep, play, socialize, chase a ball (or the mail carrier), hunt mice, exercise, or any other activities that reveal just what her energy expenditures are. Measure the total amount of food in cups for now; later on, in chapter 3, you will be able to translate that amount into calories. An important key to diagnosis, this week-long chronicle of your pet's life will also reveal much about two other contributing factors, namely:

- how bored your pet is
- your role in contributing to the problem

After you have recorded every morsel of food your dog or cat eats—even garbage or prey animals should be marked down—the total volume of food can be compared with the amount your pet should be eating. This comparison will sober you and alert you to the need for dietary reform. (Note: You will be able to determine just how much your dog or cat should be eating through conversations with your vet and through close attention to chapter 3. This amount won't be formulaic; rather, it will be based on the pet's unique metabolism.)

Again, with regard to recording your pet's activities, list clearly identifiable events such as walks, play periods, jogs, swims, or even chasing the mail carrier down the driveway. Also list periods of relative inactivity, such as sleeping, resting, being petted, being groomed, eating, or even begging. Make sure to record how long each activity lasts. Don't get too specific, however. For instance, there's no need to write, "My cat walked over to the water dish, lapped at the water, sniffed at her empty food dish, meowed plaintively, then leaped up onto the counter to lick up bread crumbs." Just write enough to be able to see each day's general pattern of activity (or lack thereof).

A small notebook is all you'll need to use for this log, though it can certainly be done on a computer, if you have one. Make it legible enough for others (such as your vet) to read. Also, instructing other members of your family to keep the log too will greatly improve the chances of getting as accurate an account as possible.

Especially important to this week-long survey is total honesty on the part of you and all your family members about the giving of treats. Confessing on paper to giving an overweight pet unnecessary treats might be a hard thing for some to do, but it is a minor discomfort when compared to the pet's health. Plus, seeing in black and white just how many indulgent tidbits are actually being secreted over to the grateful, portly pet in a day's time will help you all see one major cause of the problem. Your dog or cat's obesity will no longer be a puzzlement to you; you'll finally understand where all that extra weight has been coming from. At that point, I hope, the "charitable donations" will stop, much to the dismay of the pet.

The following is a sample day from a "control-week" log, taken from one that I kept for my own dog Louie, during the beginnings of his slim-down period. It helped me to see that Louie just wasn't getting enough exercise, due in great part to my hectic work schedule. It also helped me come to the conclusion that he was simply eating more than his slowing metabolism could handle.

MONDAY, JUNE 10

7:30 A.M.   I take Lou for a ten-minute walk, the
               first of the day.

8:30 A.M.	I feed Lou ½ cup of kibble for breakfast.
8:45 A.M.	I brush him, and trim his nails.
8:50 A.M.	Lou lies down beneath my desk for about three hours, while I work on the computer.
Noon	Lou brings me his ball. We play fetch for ten minutes.
12:15 P.M.	I leave the condo to write at a coffee shop. Lou is alone for about five hours.
5:00 P.M.	I take Lou for his second walk.
5:20 P.M.	Lou lies down beneath my desk while I do some work on the computer.
7:30 P.M.	After I eat my dinner, I give Lou his, consisting of 2½ cups of kibble and a raw egg.
7:40 P.M.	Lou lies down for a while.
8:00 P.M.	I take Lou for the third walk of the day.
8:15 P.M.	After we get back, Lou crawls underneath my bed and goes to sleep.
11:45 P.M.	I take Lou for his last walk.
12:15 A.M.	Both of us go to sleep.

As you can see, my dog had a fairly boring day, with a total of about forty-five minutes of walking and some fetching as the only energetic activities. He also spent nearly six hours at home alone, most of it probably underneath my desk, asleep. The bottom line: He did not get nearly enough exercise or mental stimulation, resulting in a sluggish metabolism and too much sleep. Looking at the log after the week was over alerted me to the fact that my inattention to Lou was the main cause of his weight gain. Less exercise than normal was the main culprit, though his slowing metabolism was also at fault. The calories contained in those three cups of dry food and the egg were now more than his nine-year-old body could burn in a day. Notice, though, that no calories came from treats; had I been giving him little tidbits during the day, Louie would have been even fatter.

A three-year-old Rottweiler mix wouldn't have a problem maintaining his ideal body weight on the amount I fed Louie. Age, therefore, is a contributor to obesity, and must be considered. My not doing so resulted in a chubby dog.

For others, the control-week log will reveal different possible causes for a pet's obesity. One client of mine used to feed her tabby treats and leftovers constantly; by the time the cat was five, he was a blimp on legs. He would meow insistently at his owner while she sat at the dinner table, demanding morsels of whatever was being eaten at the time. Pot roast, ham, bread, pasta, and even cooked carrots were dutifully and happily tossed down to the little feline in an attempt to satisfy his insatiable appetite. This went on at every meal. The owner even went so far as to prepare *a separate plate of food* for the cat, in an attempt to keep him from meowing and jumping onto the table. Incredible! When she gave me her completed control-week log, I was shocked, not so much by the amounts of table scraps fed to the cat but by the owner's candid admissions to it all. She was almost proud of it. It gave her pleasure to feed the cat, and she didn't realize that doing so was shortening the pet's life and creating a behavioral nightmare. To her credit, she recorded every morsel of meat and each baby carrot. The log was pages long. It was a miracle the poor cat hadn't exploded!

The week-long log will allow you to collect clues and evidence that point to the cause or causes of your dog or cat's weight problem. Keep it judiciously, be honest, and try to have every member of the family participate. Remember: This exercise is designed mainly to describe in detail your pet's daily routine and to show you how crucial your role is in causing or preventing your pet's obesity. Don't be surprised if you learn that the main cause of your pet's weight problem turns out to be you.

2. Owner Self-Evaluation:

Are You Causing the Problem?

Let's face it: Your dog or cat does not whip herself up a big meal whenever she's hungry. She can't drive to the pet store and buy food. She most likely can't dial the telephone and get pizza delivered at eleven P.M. All she can do is look to you for her nourishment, just as a toddler would. If we let toddlers choose their meals, they would happily decide on a menu of potato chips, candy, soda pop, and gum. Broccoli, peas, bananas, and spinach would be quite low on the list. Likewise, we would not let toddlers choose how much of a favorite food they would eat. "Yes, Mommy, I'll have twenty-three chocolate bars and five cans of cola, please."

Given that most adult dogs or cats have the reasoning capacity of a two-year-old human, it stands to reason that you also cannot let a pet decide what he will eat, how much, or when. The owner should make these decisions, ideally based on what is best for the pet, and not on the animal's desires. And most owners do just that. Or do they?

Often, the answer to this question is no. True, most owners choose what type and brand of dog or cat food they will feed their pets, based in part on advertising, palatability, and recommendations from other owners. Most owners also decide on what they think is an appropriate amount for their pets to eat. After all, it seems common sense that large pets should eat more than small pets, young ones more than old, active ones more than sedentary. So then, if most owners are solidly in charge of these aspects of feeding, why are there any fat pets at all?

The answer is that, though they think they are in charge, they are in fact not. The cat or dog often is. Pretty shocking concept? Not at all. Dogs and cats are predators, and as such have been used to manipulating their environment for millions of years. It is easier than you think: A little look or a quiet woof or meow is often all it takes to convince a loving owner to hand over a slice of cheese or a piece of pot roast. It's called *conditioned response*. Except it's not the pets who are being conditioned to respond. It's us.

The Psychology of Spoiling

What exactly do we mean when we say "you are spoiling that child," or "that kid is a spoiled brat"? Generally, we mean that the child in question is being given things that he or she has not earned or does not deserve. A spoiled child may get every toy he asks for, every piece of candy she cries for, every roller-coaster ride he demands. Giving in to a child's demands in this way is what is called spoiling. Even though we know that giving the child what he or she wants isn't necessarily the best thing to do, we do it anyway. Why? The reasons are many, but it's generally accepted that the spoiling of a child occurs because of inadequate understanding of basic child behavior, and a need by the parent to prove his or her love by giving whatever is asked for, as soon as possible. Whatever the reason, a spoiled child quickly becomes obnoxious, demanding, and unruly, and slowly but surely takes over the parent-child relationship. Often the parent is the last to know, thinking the behavior being reinforced in the child is endearing or cute.

Dog and cat owners are famous for spoiling their pets. All of us have been guilty of this to varying degrees. Who can resist the cute eyes of an eight-week-old retriever puppy, or the quiet, plaintive meow of a tiny Siamese kitten? Not many. We love them, and we are ready and willing to give whatever they ask for in return for their love and attention. After all, that's why we get pets in the first place. We want undying loyalty and companionship. So, to prove our love, we give our pets whatever they seem to be wanting at the time, be it a scratch behind the ears, a pat on the head, a cookie, or an extra spoon of food in their dinner dish. And so it begins.

Spoiling a dog or cat is an easier task than spoiling a human. We humans eventually develop some level of abstract, mature thought; they, however, remain forever two years old, with very concrete mind-sets: "When I do this, they do that." Stimulus, response. When we begin giving our pets unearned treats and attention, we set into motion a pattern of behavior that our pets understand perfectly. They quickly understand that whenever they want, they can get you to give them some food or attention. Once your cat or dog learns this lesson, he begins to take charge of the relationship. Though no pet ever got fat from too much petting, the same can't be said for food offerings. The owner who proves his or her love through the offering of food becomes an architect of pet obesity.

It starts simply enough. Your beagle ambles over to you while you are trimming the fat off a piece of steak. You give it to him, happily. He now comes into the kitchen whenever you are preparing a meal, knowing you are likely to hand over a morsel, instead of resisting his adoring gaze. You like the attention, he likes the food. Unfortunately, you have initiated a behavior that can easily lead to an overweight, spoiled dog.

Owners who are guilty of giving treats to their pets all day long are doing so because *they derive pleasure from the giving*. In an increasingly unresponsive, impersonal world, it is comforting to have a pet who responds gratefully and immediately to your offerings. What a refreshing thing: an intelligent living being paying us undivided attention! In the end, though, unearned treat giving must not be seen as an altruistic, selfless act, but rather as an attention-getting ploy designed to make *us* feel good, ultimately at the pet's expense. Understand that they do not know better, *but you do.*

There is a place for treat giving, however. When you want to reward and encourage a specific behavior such as "come" or "sit," then by all means offer up a small tasty tidbit, especially during the learning phase. As the behavior begins to become ingrained, however, it will be more strongly reinforced if you give treats only intermittently, and give physical praise the rest of the time. If a dog or cat gets a treat every time she performs a desired behavior, the process becomes too predictable, causing the pet to respond more slowly. Intermittent treat giving, on the other hand, will keep the pet on her toes; she won't really know if a treat is on its way, causing her to perform the behavior more quickly, in an attempt to find out if, this time, a little snack is coming.

In other words, treats should be given as a reward for performing a desired task. Treats should be *earned*. Treats should not be given simply because the pet is in the room.

That is a recipe not only for obesity, but for pushy, dominant behavior as well. Owners of dogs and cats who disregard this advice are unknowingly spoiling their pets in an attempt to secure their love and attention. The point is, a competent, caring, confident owner does not need to *buy* a pet's love; if treated well, the pet will love freely, without being bribed. The moral: *Ease off on the treats!*

The Leadership and Control Issue

Unfortunately, many dog and cat owners have poor control over their pets, often because of a lack of leadership. Both felines and canines instinctively understand dominant and submissive behavior, a direct throwback to life in the wild. Both strive to be at the top of the dominance hierarchy, where the strongest, biggest, most domineering animals wield power over the less remarkable, weaker, more placating animals. Though more developed in canines, cats and dogs both strive to know their places in this hierarchy, just as their wild cousins do.

When a well-meaning owner gives his or her pet whatever he wants whenever he wants, he or she is telling the pet that he is dominant and has the right to do whatever he desires. Consequently, the hapless owner develops very little control over the pet. The only way a "submissive" owner can affect a pushy, dominant pet's behavior, then, is through food bribery. Food becomes the only attention getter available. When a disobedient dog runs into the street, the only way a hapless owner thinks he or she can get him to come back is through the offering of a delectable treat. When a headstrong, indoor city cat accidentally gets outside and onto the rooftop, her frantic owner can only shake the cat food box in an attempt to get her back. A pattern develops:

The owner learns to rely on food offerings as the only means of control over the disobedient pet; and these dominant, unruly pets—smarter than we give them credit for—learn to purposely break the rules in order to receive a treat. *They actually train us.* Eventually, the owner is left with a constantly disobedient, fat pet.

Using food to obtain acceptable behavior from a dog or cat can (and often does) result in an obese pet. Owners who only use treats to elicit the desired behaviors from their pets are helping to cause the obesity problem, plain and simple.

With dogs especially, there are many other behavioral modifiers available; slices of cheese or roast beef needn't be used exclusively. Modifying a cat's behavior can be a bit more challenging; treats are often one of the only effective tools. The size and the number of treats can be drastically reduced, however, to prevent obesity from occurring.

To avoid falling into the trap of using food as your only behavior modifier, you have to learn to be the "top banana" of your little pack. Once you become the leader in your dog or cat's eyes, he will *want* to obey you, simply out of an instinctive allegiance to the pack hierarchy. They are programmed to do this; all you need do is learn how to become your pet's leader. (To do so, refer to chapter 6, Train Your Pet.) Once you learn how to be the leader of your pack, you won't need to give your pet nearly as many treats, resulting in a thinner and more responsive animal.

Like Owner, Like Pet?

In working with pet owners over the years, I have noticed a disturbing correlation between the weight of the pet and the weight of the owner. Very often, an individual with a weight problem will own a pet with the same malady. Curiously, this phenomenon applies not only to overweight individuals, but to underweight owners as well. Though not supported by clinical data, this anecdotal observation has in my experience been true too many times to be ignored. Why would this be the case?

Just as parents often imprint their eating habits upon their children, so too can owners foist them upon their pets. Individuals who find food to be a comfort and a relief from boredom or stress will often pass this trait onto their pets, as will those who shy away from food for fear of becoming fat. The pet in question either becomes obese or anorexic, through no choice of her own.

This book does not pretend to try to solve the weight problems of pet lovers; the psychological roots of compulsive overeating or anorexia in humans is far beyond the scope of any animal behaviorist. It does attempt, however, to at least make owners aware of the phenomenon of human eating habits being passed onto pets. If these habits are flawed, the pets may suffer. So, try to separate your eating habits from those of your pet, with regard to quantity and quality of food.

Stimulus Neglect

As stated in the last section, many people often eat out of boredom, when they feel there is nothing else to do but sit on the sofa, watch television, and eat potato chips all evening. When people's lives lack meaningful, stimulating activity, they often become overweight. Chronically obese persons no longer able to physically get out of the home often become even more obese, simply because there is almost nothing else they can do but eat and remain inactive.

The same can hold true for dogs and cats. When a pet

has very little to do all day, he becomes bored and listless. Inadvertently, many owners create a very humdrum existence for their pets. They get up, get ready for work, pet and feed the dog or cat (and walk a dog), and then leave for eight to ten hours, thinking that the pet will have no trouble amusing himself all day in the home or yard.

The truth is, dogs and cats crave stimulus just as much as humans. As mammals go, they are pretty high on the intelligence scale, and can go stir-crazy when not provided with some way to pass the time. Think about it: You get to interact with others of your kind all day. You can talk, laugh, walk, sing, work, eat, observe, exercise, or drive a car. What does a latchkey pug or tabby get to do? Walk around. Sniff the food dish. Nibble on food (if there is any). Drink water. Look out the window. Jump onto the dresser. Bark at the UPS person. Sleep. Sleep some more. Smell the golden retriever down the block. Try to get into the garbage. Chew on a toy. Chase and eat a spider. Sleep.

Not very stimulating. But this is status quo for most pets in the country. These bored, highly social animals, with no meaningful attention or activity in their daily lives, have little else to do but eat. And so, for the cats and dogs whose owners have left big bowls of food down, entertainment becomes *eating*. Pick a little. Then a little more. Then more and more, until by three P.M., the dish is empty. Upon coming home and noticing the empty dish, most owners think, "Gee, Fido seems to never have any food left when I get home," or "I must not be leaving enough food down for Felix each day." So, in response, the owner leaves more food, then more and more. The pet, having nothing else to do, eats it all, out of boredom. You could put a wheelbarrow of food down, and some pets would still finish it off. It has less to do with hunger, and much more to do with stimulus neglect.

No social creature wants to be left alone all day, with nothing at all to do. If I locked you up in a room every day with nothing but a crate of cupcakes and a *TV Guide*, not only would you become obese, but you would also know everything there is to know about programming on every channel. You'd be an expert, able to recite the Thursday night lineup off the top of your head, for every network. And you'd also be the world's most knowledgeable connoisseur of cupcakes—their consistency, their flavor, their nutritional value. You would be, in other words, quite mad.

Being left home alone for many hours can be a very stressful, boring, monotonous experience for a pet. Many potential dog owners do not consider this when purchasing a pet; they just know that *they* desire the attentions and love of a puppy, and act upon those feelings, not realizing that, especially for a puppy, being alone all day can be agonizing and developmentally detrimental. Even cats, much more able to deal with solitude, crave attention, either from other cats or from humans. Many pet cats, particularly those neutered at an early age, tend to maintain a rather juvenile persona throughout life; they never really graduate from a "litter" mentality, a mind-set that calls for and allows much more socialization than normal for an adult, unneutered cat. Consequently, these cats, when left alone all day, can become as stressed and bored as a dog. Food for these pets becomes a nursemaid, a companion, a way to pass the time.

You the owner are responsible for the health and welfare of your dog or cat. You are the one who has set up the parameters of her day. If you provide your pet with nothing but a roof and a bucket of food, then you aren't being fair. It's not up to the pet to amuse herself; it is up to you. Remember: Your pet has the reasoning capacity of a two-year-old child.

Would you leave your toddler at a day care facility that provided absolutely no thought-provoking, enjoyable activities, but instead simply provided food and shelter? I think not. But that is what most owners provide for their pets.

Realistically, you simply cannot stay home and amuse your pet all day. But there are things you can do to help stimulate your pet and create a happier mind-set, one that is not so fixated on food. Often something as simple as leaving a radio on and tuned to a news station can be extremely comforting to a pet, as can leaving a television on in a closed room, creating the illusion that you are home. These and many more stimulating, stress-relieving techniques are discussed at length in chapter 5, Behavioral Enrichment Programs. Also, in chapter 3, Diet, the drawbacks of free-feeding are discussed in detail, and its alternatives are given. Remember that free-feeding ultimately contributes mightily to dog or cat obesity. Remember also that food itself is not supposed to be a toy or a stimulating activity; it's supposed to be *food*. Interesting activities burn calories; food *is* calories. Do not fall into the trap of thinking that you have to leave a latchkey pet with a heaping bowl of food to pass the time!

Evaluate Your Role: First the Cause, and Then the Solution

Look carefully at your control-week log. Search for patterns, and pay close attention to the following:

- Is your cat or dog left alone for more than five or six hours at a time?

- Does your pet rarely get to socialize with other humans or animals?

- Are there no regularly scheduled play and/or training periods each day?

- Is the pet being given more treats than you initially realized?

- Are you free-feeding?

- Are the portions you give your dog or cat more than what the food manufacturer recommends for your pet's weight and age?

- Are the portions more than what your vet says is needed?

- Are there no toys or chews made available to your pet during the day?

- Are you giving your pet lots of fat-laden table scraps?

- Do you reward your pet's begging with a treat?

- Do you give your pet unearned treats?

- Does your cat or dog spend an inordinate amount of time asleep each day?

- Do you regularly try to distract your pet from performing an undesirable behavior by feeding him?

- Is your pet destructive while home alone?

If you answered yes to more than a few of these questions, chances are you are responsible for your pet's overweight condition. Owning up to your responsibility as an owner is the first crucial step on the road to bringing down your pet's weight; without admitting your culpability, there won't be much hope of success. We are the stewards of the domestic pets of the world. By bringing them into our homes, we have removed nature's controls. Remember: There are no fat wolves or tigers!

Once you have admitted your role in the matter, you can begin to change, and in so doing change your pet's lifestyle, which is the key to weight loss. You have to begin to teach your dog or cat that there's a whole world of interesting things to do besides eating and sleeping; food is not the only joy in life!

To that end, the upcoming chapter will deal specifically with diet, what is right for your pet, and how to properly adapt your dog or cat to a new feeding regimen. Rather than giving one hard-and-fast way to feed your pet, this chapter will provide you with various feeding options, based on the idea that, like humans, dogs and cats are individuals with unique needs and desires. This is perhaps the most important of the book's points, and it may have more of an effect on your pet's weight than all the others.

3. Diet

Adapt Your Pet's Eating Habits to Fit His Metabolism and Lifestyle

Food is fuel, true, but it means much more than that to us, to our pets, and to all animals on the planet. Obtaining food is for most a quest, a constant struggle, a life or death search that goes on from the cradle to the grave. Procuring nourishment is probably (along with reproduction) one of the most powerful drives existing in nature, one that shapes the actions of every living thing on the planet. A hawk soars not to be majestic, but to search for a morning meal that might be scurrying across the warming desert floor. A moray eel lurks in deep crevices not out of shyness, but to lunge out from the darkness suddenly and sink his fangs into some oblivious fish. A tiger moves low and slow through the high Siberian grass not to flaunt her stalking abilities, but to ambush an unsuspecting deer feeding peacefully in the evening sun. A wolf in the Alaskan tundra runs not for the love of running, but to catch, kill, and eat a young elk separated from his mother.

As discussed earlier, nature is cleverly able to maintain a distinct balance between calories in and calories out for most members of the animal kingdom. If for some reason that balance is ever disturbed, sickness and death usually follow.

For humans and domesticated animals, however, that is no longer the case. Food is no longer difficult to find; predators have been vanquished, and disease has been greatly diminished. For humans, even the strength of the food drive seems to have been somewhat reduced over the eons, at least in comparison to our canine and feline friends. We are now able to collect in large groups and be around vast amounts of food (as when at a supermarket), without becoming aggressive, territorial, or possessive.

But, this is not the case for cats and dogs, as we've said. Both remain predatory at heart; both remain forever excited at the prospect of food. When provided to them, most do not hesitate to eat quickly, hungrily. They are also much more protective of food than we are; observe what happens when one dog approaches another while she eats: "Grrrrr . . . get outta my face, mutt!" Most humans have overcome that reaction, even when the food in question is delectable.

Harness the Food Drive

What, then, can we do about this food drive imbalance that our domestic dogs and cats experience? Trainers have known the answer to that for hundreds of years: They harness it and redirect it into a behavioral medium. They get animals (including dogs and cats) to channel their drives into any number of activities. Performing a trick in exchange for a small treat becomes as stimulating to the domesticated pet as the chasing down and eating of prey are to a wolf or leopard.

I am not saying that you need to teach your dog or cat

specific tricks to combat obesity. What I am saying is that you need to put more attention into expanding your pet's repertoire of behaviors, and in getting him to think not only in terms of dinner. The food drive can be, in other words, co-opted: Instead of giving large meals without an expectation of something in return, you must start thinking about a more balanced relationship, one in which your dog or cat begins to understand that he must in some way *work* for his food, just as wild animals do.

Training your pet will be discussed in detail in chapter 6. Chapter 5 will also delve into this area, with special focus on expanding a pet's repertoire of behaviors to create a more natural, healthy, inquisitive mind-set. For now, understand that *the food drive of your pet can be redirected* and used as a tool to open her up to new behaviors and experiences besides eating, sleeping, and being bored.

Differing Food Types and Their Effects on Your Pet's Weight

Most of us have come to rely on commercially available pet foods as our pets' main source of nutrition. Most provide adequate nutrients, and many deliver an optimal balance of needed essentials. But in addition to these manufactured brands, many owners are beginning to choose another option: in-home preparation of their pet's food. Though more time-consuming and expensive, this method of feeding has its advantages, as we shall see.

Commercially Prepared Dry Pet Food

The most widely used type of pet food today, dry pet food is the most convenient and the most economical, on a pound-for-pound basis. With a very low water content, it has a fairly long shelf life and will stay fresher longer when in your pet's bowl than will other forms of food. Dry food also tends to be slightly more abrasive than canned, semimoist, or home-cooked foods, and therefore may help clean your pet's teeth. (In my opinion this claim has been exaggerated by the pet food companies, however. Research does not point to a profound decrease in tooth decay among dogs and cats raised solely on dry food.)

Generally, dry pet food can be divided into two broad categories: supermarket brands and pet shop brands. Supermarket foods, sold by the millions of bags each year, tend to be on the whole less expensive than what is available in pet shops. These foods also usually contain higher levels of preservatives, coloring agents, and taste enhancers, and they can have measurable levels of pesticide residue, as well as residual amounts of antibiotics and hormones used in the raising of the meat that goes into the mixture. Cheaper brands may contain low-quality meat and meat by-products not approved for human consumption by the United States Department of Agriculture. Meat by-products can legally include beaks, feathers, bones, heads, organs, skin, and even fecal material. It is even perfectly legal for dog and cat food companies to use diseased or dying animals in their foods. Would you want your dog or cat to eat something you would never consider eating?

Most of the big brand-name dry foods, however, now produce a quality product that will promote good health in your pet. If you choose this option, you can be assured that your pet is getting adequate nutrition at a reasonable price. Just make certain the supermarket dry food you choose uses real meat instead of meat by-products.

Pet shop dry foods normally have a higher degree of quality, both in the ingredients and in the processes used to create the product. Because they are manufactured in smaller batches and sold at substantially higher prices, these foods can be and normally are made with better ingredients, including better meat, fresher grains, fewer preservatives, and a complete spectrum of the necessary vitamins and minerals. Because many of these foods have little or no preservatives, however, their shelf life will be much shorter than those of supermarket foods. The formula of the food itself is often more carefully thought out and monitored with pet shop dry foods than with supermarket brands; percentages of protein, fat, carbohydrates, and other ingredients are carefully adjusted to match the unique needs of the pet, whatever the age. Overall, pet shop dry foods are recommended, if you don't mind paying thirty to thirty-five dollars for a forty-pound bag.

Whether you decide to use a supermarket or a pet shop dry pet food, make sure it has:

- the proper nutrient balance for the age of your pet
- a freshness date somewhere on the package, as well as the manufacturer's guarantee that the product is nutritionally complete
- meat as the first ingredient
- whole, cooked grains instead of grain "fractions," such as peanut hulls, empty grain husks, or even sawdust

- as few artificial ingredients and preservatives as possible

Canned Food

Canned pet food can provide adequate nutrition for your dog or cat, and as an added bonus it has a very long shelf life. Available in a wide variety of quality levels, this type of food can be fed alone or as a supplement to dry food. Canned pet food can be primarily meat based, or it can have a cereal content high enough to require grains to be listed as the primary ingredient. For dogs and cats, primarily carnivorous by nature, the food they eat should have meat as its main ingredient, so try to avoid canned foods that are mostly grain based.

Canned food contains approximately 50 to 70 percent water. This has its good and bad sides. The good side is that these percentages closely resemble food in the wild and as such will supply your dog or cat with more moisture than will dry food. This can help prevent kidney disease caused by a chronic lack of water in the pet's diet. The extra water can also make elimination easier and more regular. On the bad side, the high water content makes canned food much more expensive and less nutritious on a pound-for-pound basis. You end up paying for water instead of food. Also, canned food can contribute to tooth decay slightly more than dry food because wetter food is a more supportive medium for bacteria. The effects of this are negligible, though, especially if you see your vet regularly and get your pet's teeth cleaned.

As in dry pet foods, the quality of canned food varies considerably, with price often being the tip-off. Cheap supermarket canned foods have the same drawbacks as cheap dry foods: a poor meat source and a high percentage of poor-quality grains, preservatives, and other undesirable ingredients. Pet shops carry higher quality brands of canned food, at a higher price. As a rule, try to avoid canned food that costs less than one dollar per eight-ounce can.

In addition to being an adequate source of nutrition on its own, canned food can also be used as a supplement to dry food, increasing its palatability and water content. Many owners simply mix a few tablespoons into the kibble, which often gets a finicky cat or dog to eat all of his meal in a shorter time.

Semimoist Food

This type of pet food is an alternative to canned or dry. Lighter and easier to store, these burger-type foods are very palatable to most pets. They are on the expensive side, however, and often contain high amounts of preservatives, artificial colorings, binders, and sugar—ingredients needed to give the food its meatlike texture. Though capable of providing adequate nutrition, semimoist food is probably the least nutritionally desirable of the commercially available foods.

Home-Cooked Food

As stated earlier, more and more dog and cat owners are beginning to appreciate the benefits of preparing their pet's food right in their own kitchens. Using fresh, raw, or lightly cooked meats, cooked whole grains, cooked vegetables, and various other ingredients, many caring owners with time on their hands prepare meals for their dogs and cats that are not only tasty, but also superior to commercial foods in several ways. In addition to being fresh, home-cooked pet food is free of artificial ingredients and potentially harmful chemicals such as pesticides, hormones, antibiotics, and preservatives. The meat used is generally only lightly cooked or raw, assuring that it contains the highest amounts possible of amino and fatty acids, protein, vitamins, and minerals; commercial foods are often subjected to high cooking temperatures for long periods, rendering their nutrients less beneficial. The meat used in home-cooked pet food need not be cooked, by the way, provided it is fresh; the digestive tracts of dogs and cats are designed to deal with raw meat much more efficiently than our own, due in great part to stronger digestive acids and enzymes. If that doesn't sit well with you, though, lightly cooking the meat won't be a problem for your pet.

The drawbacks to home cooking are few but noteworthy. First, it is more time intensive than just buying a bag or can of pet food. You have to spend nearly as much time cooking for Fido or Felix as for yourself; even cooking larger batches of pet food and freezing for use later on takes time, both in preparation and in thawing and reheating individual portions. You have to shop more often and acquire the ingredients in different areas of the store, or sometimes even in separate stores. Also, home-cooked pet food is much more similar to human food in appearance and aroma than is commercial pet food. This can cause certain pets to begin begging at the dinner table in response to the same type of food being served there as in their bowls. And begging, of course, is one of the prime culprits in pet obesity (primarily because owners give in to the requests).

Analysis of the Different Food Types with Respect to Weight Gain

Any food you feed your dog or cat can make him fat. If you fed your pet fifteen cups of rice each day (poor thing), he would become overweight. Certain types of food do tend to be more caloric than others, however.

Of the four basic classes of pet food just discussed, dry food tends to be on the whole the most calorie dense, for the simple reason that it contains the least amount of water on a per-pound basis and is therefore the easiest to overfeed. This is one of the main reasons my dog Louie gained weight; he tends to eat a mostly dry-food diet, with some meat and other supplements added in. I am currently considering switching him over to the senior version of his food, one that contains about 10 percent less calories per pound than what he's used to. Senior or "lite" versions of pet foods are very prevalent today; nearly every brand of dry, canned, or semi-moist pet food is now available in this reduced-calorie version. The advantage of switching to one of these foods is simple: It allows the pet to consume the same volume of food while taking in fewer calories. This permits the animal to feel satiated, yet still lose weight. This feeling of fullness is important to pets, and especially to dogs; pets that do not reach this point often constantly beg, or else get into some form of mischief such as stealing food from other pets or raiding the garbage.

Foods that are very high in fat also tend to be highly caloric. Fatty meats, oils, and eggs or other dairy products can cause the calorie levels of your pet's meal to go through the roof if not used in moderation. Saturated fats, which are animal derived, are particularly fattening. They should whenever possible be replaced by mono- or polyunsaturated fats such as fish, olive, canola, flax seed, safflower, or sesame seed oil. These oils are lower in calories and provide the pet with essential fatty acids and vitamins and give them energy.

Canned and semimoist pet foods do have slightly fewer calories per pound than dry food, but they can often contain higher quantities of fat as well as sugar (used as a binder not as a flavor enhancer), which can increase the calorie count substantially. Owners feeding canned food to their obese pets should try to find a brand with little or no added sugar. Those feeding semimoist food will be hard-pressed to find one without sugar, as it is used to give the food its characteristic texture. If your pet is at all overweight, I advise abandoning the use of semimoist food in favor of canned or dry.

What type of food you feed your dog or cat depends on the pet's personality and on your time and budget. You can tell if the food is an appropriate match to your pet's constitution, though, by observing the pet itself. First, look at her stools: Are they relatively small, medium in color, and fairly firm? Or are they very large, lighter in color than the food itself, and runny? The former is in general more healthy and reflects good digestion and health. Second, your cat or dog's coat is always a good indicator of her general health. A glossy, fresh-smelling coat is normally indicative of good health, whereas a dry, brittle, oily, or odorous coat often points to poor health, or at the very least a poor diet.

Determine Ideal Caloric Needs: Just How Much Is Right for Your Pet?

Though every pet is unique in his nutritional needs, certain standards can be established with regard to just how many calories an adult cat or dog should take in each day to maintain metabolism and function without weight loss or gain. The following are broad guidelines listing minimum caloric intake for dogs and cats of varying sizes and ages. Again, these figures are average amounts; the actual figure for your pet will vary according to your pet's unique metabolism, age, and activity level. Note that smaller pets actually have higher per-pound calorie needs than larger ones, and puppies and kittens have a higher need than adults.

Daily caloric requirements for adult dogs

Under 10 lb:	approximately 50–60 calories per pound body weight
10–35 lb:	approximately 30–40 calories per pound body weight
35–65 lb:	approximately 20–25 calories per pound body weight
Over 70 lb:	approximately 20 calories per pound body weight

Daily caloric requirements for puppies

Under 4 months:	approximately 80–100 calories per pound body weight
4–6 months:	approximately 65–75 calories per pound body weight
6–12 months:	approximately 50–65 calories per pound body weight

Daily caloric requirements for adult cats

| Under 10 lb: | approximately 40–50 calories per pound body weight |
| Over 10 lb: | approximately 35–45 calories per pound body weight |

Daily caloric requirements for kittens

Under 4 months:	approximately 90–125 calories per pound body weight
4–6 months:	approximately 65–80 calories per pound body weight
6–9 months:	approximately 50–60 calories per pound body weight

As stated earlier, pet foods vary in their caloric values. Generally, the following figures closely approximate how many calories each type of food contains *per cup*. This figure can vary substantially, however, according to the individual formula and the food's purpose. For instance, puppy and kitten foods normally can contain 50 percent more calories than do adult foods, whereas senior or "lite" foods contain 20 to 30 percent less calories. The caloric value for home-cooked pet food can vary tremendously, according to ingredients. For instance, adding a whole egg or a tablespoon of olive oil to a meal can boost the calorie levels by 20 to 30 percent.

Dry:	approximately 400 calories per cup
Semimoist:	approximately 250 calories per cup
Canned:	approximately 150 calories per cup
Home-cooked:	varies widely according to formula; refer to a paperback calorie counter for exact calories per cup

Using these figures as our guideline, let's calculate how many calories should be in some average pets' diets. A typical three-year-old golden retriever, for instance, whose ideal weight might be somewhere between sixty and seventy pounds, should be eating about 1,500–1,800 calories per day, provided she is moderately active. In contrast, an adult toy poodle, whose weight might be only eight to ten pounds, should be consuming about 500–600 calories per day. An adult tabby weighing in at about ten pounds would need to take in about 500 calories per day, whereas a big brute of a cat weighing fifteen pounds or so would need about 675 calories to maintain himself.

These figures are for dogs and cats who are not overweight. Pets who are taking in approximately these amounts of calories but are obese are obviously not metabolizing the calories efficiently, probably due to a lack of activity. For these pets, a 15 to 20 percent reduction in calories is in order. Anything more than this, however, could lead to an inadequate supply of essential nutrients. Weight loss must be a gradual process. A loss of more than 2 percent of the pet's current body weight per week should not be allowed.

If you feed your pet lots of human table scraps, it might be a good idea to pick up a calorie-counter paperback book and actually calculate the number of calories you are unknowingly adding to her diet each day. You might be shocked by what you discover. For instance, only one ounce of pot roast has nearly a hundred calories; one slice of American cheese has nearly the same. For a small to medium-sized dog or cat, this treat alone could amount to nearly a quarter of her allotted daily calories.

Using the above guidelines and the information contained in your control-week log, try to calculate how many calories your overweight pet is consuming each day, including treats and table scraps. Using the general "calories per cup" figures from above (or, if available, the food manufacturer's calorie information), as well as the information derived from a calorie-counter book with regard to treats and scraps, come as close as you can to the exact number. Biscuit-type treats normally have the same caloric value as the identical amount of dry food, and softer treats are similar to semimoist food figures. If your total calorie count is substantially higher than the calorie guidelines above for your pet, then you know where much of the problem lies.

Common Feeding Mistakes and Their Solutions

With some pets, it doesn't matter how often or how much you feed them: They just don't get fat. Some dogs and cats are simply blessed with a fast metabolism and find use for every calorie eaten. Other pets are self-regulating: When they have had enough, they stop eating, regardless if there is still food available to them. If you have one of these pets, go over and kiss him on the nose, right now! These are rare animals; normally, the presence of excess food spells trouble, and leads to obesity.

The following are the most common feeding mistakes that both dog and cat owners make with their pets, both at feeding time and during the day, with respect to treats and randomly offered table scraps. All of them can and do contribute to obesity in pets; you may find that you are guilty of one, two, or many of them. Even making one of these mistakes with a cat or dog prone to weight gain can result in an obese pet. (Note: I differentiate between treats and table scraps in this way: Treats are small tidbits of food given to the pet at various times throughout the day, for a variety of reasons, whereas table scraps are leftover or unwanted *human* food given to the pet either during or right after the family has eaten dinner.)

Free-Feeding

Often used by owners who are away from the home for extended periods during the day, free-feeding involves leaving a fairly large quantity of food (usually the equivalent of two or three individual meals) in the pet's bowl in the morning in hopes that the dog or cat will pick at it throughout the day. In some cases, owners actually invest in "auto-feeders," automatic feeding contraptions consisting of a bowl and a large reservoir of food above it; food is slowly metered into the bowl throughout the day as the pet eats. The reservoir on some of these auto-feeders can hold upward of six to ten meals at a time. Cat owners who regularly leave for days at a time often resort to this device; as most cats can instinctively use a litter box, they can be left alone for relatively long periods in this manner.

Owners who do free-feed have no way of determining just how much food their pets are really eating on a daily basis. There is instead a constant, free-flowing supply of calories heading into the dish and the pet. Without knowing precisely how much food your overweight cat or dog is eating each day, how can you possibly help her lose weight?

The solution to this problem is simple. Instead of leaving large amounts of food down at all times, change over to a regular feeding schedule. Both cats and dogs will benefit tremendously from you doing so, not only in terms of calorie management, but also in "resetting" the pet's food drive instinct, a tactic that will aid you in predicting when and how much your pet should eat. Even for those owners who are gone for eight to ten hours per day, adapting a pet to a regular feeding schedule is easily accomplished. Feed your dog or cat twice each day, once before you leave in the morning (often a smaller meal) and then once in the evening, preferably right after you have eaten dinner. After doing so, you will quickly find your pet looking forward to feeding time more than he used to while under a free-feeding regimen. This renewed anticipation of food is the way a dog or cat should react; by restoring this instinct, you will also make your pet more trainable, as the food drive plays a key role in adapting existing behaviors or in creating new ones. And don't worry: Your pet will not starve during the day. Just make sure fresh water is readily available all the time.

With regard to puppies and kittens, who usually need to eat three times each day, consider having a neighbor or friend come over at noon each day to give the pet her midday feeding. It must be said, however, that keeping a puppy all by herself all day is a bad idea, for several reasons. First, a puppy, more than an adult animal or even a kitten, needs socialization and guidance on a nearly constant basis until well past six months of age. Without a diligent owner present, a puppy will never learn proper house-training etiquette, will in all likelihood become destructive, and may become severely antisocial due to the absence of contact with humans or other animals. There just is no excuse for leaving a puppy home alone all day. Even leaving her in the yard, which prevents destruction of the home, will do nothing for establishing proper house-training habits or for promoting proper socialization.

Caring for a kitten is not nearly as demanding; kittens are almost always litter box trained by the time you get them and are by nature less needy when it comes to socialization. Still, it's a good idea to feed a kitten on a regular schedule right from the beginning to encourage the proper eating habits early on. It is also a good idea to have two kittens home alone instead of one, as this will help them pass the time and quell any feelings of loneliness. This idea won't work for puppies, however; two puppies home alone just equals twice the trouble. And if you think that leaving a puppy home with an older dog is the answer, think again. When was the last time you saw a five-year-old German shepherd house-train a three-month-old shepherd puppy?

Feeding Too Much Food

Though it sounds overly simplistic, some owners simply feed their pets too much food each day. I was guilty of this myself with Louie. I continued to feed him the same amount of food without realizing that advancing age and a reduction in exercise had slowed down his metabolism. What used to be the perfect amount of food before soon became excessive.

The bad news is that no mathematical formula exists to help you decide exactly how much to feed your dog or cat. That would be possible only if your pet were a static, predictable engine, using the same amount of fuel every day and performing the same amount of work. That just isn't the case. Instead, much like ourselves, our pets have varying degrees of activity, widely ranging metabolisms, and different appetite levels. A toy poodle, for instance, has a proportionately higher metabolic rate than does a bullmastiff, just as a lithe Cornish rex does over a larger Norwegian forest cat. A sleepy old Clumber spaniel moves more slowly than a young pointer; a spry Siamese runs rings around an ancient Manx. Because of these inherent differences, it is nearly impossible for a book to predict exactly how much food your individual pet will need to not gain weight.

That said, some very basic guidelines can be given. First, refer to the figures stating the average caloric requirements of your pet. For instance, let's assume you have a four-year-old Labrador retriever. According to the figures, an adult dog weighing approximately sixty-five pounds will need to take in about twenty to twenty-five calories per pound per day to fuel his basic metabolism. If we now do the math, that works out to between 1,300 and 1,625 calories per day, *roughly speaking*. These are not figures carved in stone, but rather starting points for you and your pet. Now, checking the figures for calories per cup of food, we see that, for dry food, there are roughly four hundred calories per cup (a figure that can vary widely depending on brand and formula). That would mean that this four-year-old Labrador retriever would need to eat about three and a quarter to just over four cups of dry food per day to maintain his body weight. The same dog would need to eat at least five cups of semimoist food, or nearly nine cups of canned. Though it sounds like a lot, these would be typical amounts for an active, fairly young retriever. Of course a dog used to swimming a few hours each day or retrieving ducks or tennis balls for hours would need more food. These numbers are simply a place to start. If your pet gains weight on them, lower the amount.

The same calculations can be done for a cat. Let's say you own a two-year-old tabby, weighing about eleven pounds. The average calories consumed per pound body weight for this pet would be between thirty-five and forty-five calories. Doing the math, this cat would need to take in between 385 and 495 calories per day, or about a cup of dry food, nearly two cups of semimoist, or around three cups of canned.

Again, these are just rough calculations, designed to give you a reference point. Your cat or dog may need appreciably more or less. Only trial and error will determine for sure. But by metering out a precise amount each day and weighing the pet once each week, you will quickly be able to tell if you are on the right track.

When measuring your overweight pet's food, it's a good idea to use an actual measuring cup, at least in the beginning. Many owners are shocked to discover that a cup of food is substantially less than they thought. One cup, or eight ounces (by volume), is not that much food, and could actually fit inside the palm of a large person's hand. And no, a coffee cup is not a valid cup; it's closer to two cups! You would be surprised to find how many owners mistakenly use a coffee cup to measure their pet's food, inadvertently feeding nearly twice the suggested amount.

These feeding approximations are for adult pets of normal weight. For pets that are overweight, you should reduce the amount by about 15 to 20 percent at first to encourage a slow but sure weight loss. When used in conjunction with exercise and other activities, this should be sufficient to take the weight off within a few months. Remember: You should not put any dog or cat on a crash diet, unless specified by your veterinarian. An abrupt and drastic cut in calories could easily create health problems more serious than the initial weight concerns. As in humans, a slow, steady reduction is the smarter course.

Pets under one year of age will of course need more calories per pound than adult animals (see calorie needs for puppies and kittens). Luckily, most kittens and puppies are active enough to avoid becoming clinically obese. Owners still overfeed their young pets, however, a mistake that can lead to overly rapid growth, which can in turn cause structural abnormalities. Play it safe. Follow the basic caloric guidelines and talk to your veterinarian to find out what is correct for your little one.

Dogs and cats over seven or eight years of age will need to eat fewer calories than their younger counterparts. Again, in my dog Louie's case, he now takes in about 20 percent less calories than when he was a young buck. As with a younger pet, knowing just how much food to feed an older dog or cat will be a function of trial and error. Just remember to weigh the pet each week, and discuss the matter with your veterinarian if questions arise.

Some pets react badly to seeing the volume of food they are used to eating each day suddenly decrease by 15 to 20 percent. Both dogs and cats are creatures of habit and can become upset and troubled by any major change in the environment. For instance, many pets run away soon after their owners have moved to another home in a different neighborhood. The pet desires to be in the old place, with its particular scents and goings-on. When a pet's food volume is suddenly decreased, some pets can and do react unfavorably, acting out in various ways from vocalizing to being destructive or moody. To prevent this you should attempt to lower the calories present but not the actual volume of the food in the dish, if at all possible. You can do this easily by removing 20 to 25 percent of the pet's normal food and then replacing it with a food of much lower caloric value. For instance, if my obese dog were eating four cups of dry food per day, I might take away one cup of dry food and replace it with a cup of brown rice, cooked green beans, or some other high-fiber, nutritious, low-calorie food. Taking away the one cup of dry food would subtract about four hundred calories; replacing it with the rice or cooked vegetable would add only fifty to one hundred calories. The net loss would be three hundred calories per day, even though the pet would feel as if she were eating the same as before. Another way of accomplishing the same thing is to switch your overweight dog or cat to a lower-calorie senior or "lite" food. Though providing the pet with the same volume, it would contain fewer calories per cup, thereby reducing the pet's total caloric intake each day. Pets with very high food drives will respond much better to these calorie-reducing methods than to simply getting less food. By using these strategies, you will reduce your pet's weight without creating any additional stress in his life.

One more precautionary word about overfeeding: A condition known as *bloat*, or *gastric torsion*, can occur in larger dog breeds who are being fed overly large meals. Often fatal, this condition is thought to be brought on when the dog eats one very large meal and then drinks a large quantity of water and exercises soon after. Gases from the digestive process can build up rapidly, causing a twisting or torsional phenomenon in the stomach. This twisting can cut off major blood vessels, which can quickly lead to shock and death if not treated by a veterinarian immediately. The easiest way to avoid this in the larger dog breeds is to feed smaller, more frequent meals, and to keep the pet from exercising for an hour or so after eating. Also, soak the larger breed's dry food in water for ten minutes before feeding. This will cause expansion to occur *outside* the dog's stomach. Feeding frequency is addressed in detail in the next section; for now, just be aware that how much you feed your pet can actually seriously affect her immediate health.

Feeding Only One Time Each Day

Many dogs and cats have no problem eating just one meal per day. This is not surprising, as wild dogs and cats rarely eat more than once each day and can often go days without a meal. Their bodies and metabolisms are designed to cope with being in a feast-or-famine environment. When a meal finally does come along, both wild cats and dogs take full advantage of the situation, taking in as much as they can to prepare for another possible period of deprivation. This infrequent eating schedule serves to strengthen the wild animal's food drive; any much-needed and enjoyable event that occurs infrequently will only increase the desire for that event. You enjoy eating lobster in part because you do so rarely. If you had it for breakfast, lunch, and dinner, it would probably lose some of its appeal.

When an obese cat or dog is fed only one large meal per day, several things happen. First, the pet can often become overly stimulated by the event because he has been waiting twenty-four hours for it to occur. Dogs especially can become extremely animated and hyperactive at this much-anticipated time; this highlight of their day stimulates them into an almost frenzied mind-set. Feeding this type of pet only once per day, then, only serves to reinforce their already inflated food drive, as well as encourage uncontrollable behavior.

It is well known among animal trainers that infrequently reinforcing a behavior actually encourages that behavior more than consistent and frequent rewards do. In other words, if I want to encourage my pet to really like playing with a particular stuffed toy, the last thing I should do is make that toy available to the pet all the time. Instead, I should bring the toy out infrequently, when I want to support the playing behavior. Making it always available would eventually desensitize the dog or cat to its presence. In this way, only feeding an obese pet once each day instead of two or three times a day heightens that animal's desire for food.

An additional problem with feeding once per day occurs with large-breed dogs. As we said, bloat, thought to be caused by the pet eating too much food at one time, can kill a dog quickly and painfully. Breaking the pet's daily food ration into two or three feedings will help prevent this often fatal disorder from occurring. Luckily, cats do not seem to suffer from this malady and so do not require multiple meals for this reason. They can be just as frenzied about eating once per day, though, and would do better to eat more often.

The solution to this problem is simple. Just feed your obese pet at least two or three times per day instead of just once. Take the daily amount of food you calculated your pet should be eating and split it into numerous smaller feedings. By feeding your obese pet more often, you will eventually help to lower the strength of her food drive, resulting in less food eaten and less of a fixation on eating. This will allow your dog or cat to become interested in other activities that will stimulate her mind and body, allowing her to feel more complete and not so frantic about dinnertime.

Another way to make the volume of your pet's food seem larger in the case of dry food is to soak it in warm water for ten minutes before serving. Dry food will nearly double in apparent volume when prepared this way, giving the pet the feeling of real satiation without increasing calories. An added benefit of this technique is the increased water being ingested, which can help flush out the pet's bladder and aid in overall digestion and health. Cats that eat an exclusively dry-food diet can really benefit from this technique because it will help reduce the amount of mineral crystallization that occurs in the bladder and kidneys, preventing all manner of urinary tract disorders.

Too Many Treats

Where to start, where to start. Simply put, next to feeding your dog or cat too much food at feeding time, the most common reason a pet becomes overweight is too many treats offered to him throughout the day. Owners of both dogs and cats are guilty of this, though dog owners tend to be more so due to the fact that canines are more easily trained, more sociable, and often more skilled at begging than cats.

It's fun to give treats or table scraps to our pets. It lends a nurturing feeling to the relationship; many of us get pets, in fact, out of an instinctive parental need to nurture something. That's a fine motivation, until it begins to adversely affect your pet's health and behavior.

Continuing to give treats all day to an obese pet ceases to be nurturing and instead becomes a selfish act that makes the owner feel in control, important, and loved. The problem is amplified when the pet quickly learns that skillful, well-timed begging will result in more goodies. As we said, they in effect train us to meter out food to them simply by appealing to our generous natures and soft hearts. Understand that in doing so you may be dooming your overweight pet to a sickly, uncomfortable, and shortened life.

The solution is simple. Whatever treats are given to the dog or cat during the day *must be included in the pet's total food allocation for the day*. In other words, if your beagle needs to limit her caloric intake to 850 calories per day to lose weight, then the treats given must be included in that number. You simply cannot feed the dog 850 calories of food each day and then offer her another 400 calories in the form of cheese, meat, bread, or cookies; if you do this, she will continue to gain weight. If you insist on giving treats, then lower the food allocation by the same number of calories contained in the treats.

Treats are useful when attempting to train a dog or cat to perform some act that is beneficial, entertaining, or necessary to the pet's survival. Having your pet come to you, for instance, is a behavior that is both convenient and potentially vital. If your dog is wandering into a busy street, for example, you must have the ability to get him to come to you instantly so he will get out of the road. Even having an indoor/outdoor cat come to you when you desire is handy, especially when you need to get her inside for the night, or for her dinner. Using tasty treats to initiate and perfect a behavior, then, is perfectly justifiable. Giving them out to your pet continually, all day, for no reason, is not.

When using treats to teach your pet a new behavior, you should give the pet the smallest possible piece; instead of giving your bulldog an entire slice of American cheese for coming in out of the rain, give him a half-inch square of cheese. The dog will still love it, and that one slice of cheese will last several training sessions instead of one hungry canine second. Likewise, when training your cat (which is very possible, by the way) use a tiny amount of cat food on the end of a stick or spoon, instead of a heaping tablespoon of something fattening. Though cats normally respond only to food rewards, remember that dogs will also perform for praise from you, the pack leader. As soon as you have a dog performing the desired behavior, start weaning her off treats and onto praise.

Another way to reduce the amount of treats given to your pet each day is to establish this basic rule: All treats must be earned. Don't just give your pet a treat for no good reason; get him to do something to earn it. Just a "sit" or "come" will do; even behaving calmly and respectfully is enough to earn a tasty bit of something. But do not reward pets for no reason. If you do, they will expect it all the time, and you will most likely oblige.

In general, if you have an obese pet, try not to rely on giving her treats all day. Be sparing, include them in the daily calorie count, and substitute praise whenever possible. Also, be sure to have all family members adopt these new rules. What's the sense of you reforming if no one else will?

Wrong Type of Food

Some owners continue to feed their pets the same types, brands, and amounts of food for the pet's entire life. This is often a mistake. Take our own human experience as an example: When we were eighteen years old, we could eat all day without gaining an ounce. At forty, however, eating the same number of calories each day would surely result in weight gain. I know it does with me, at least!

The same holds true for dogs and cats. For example, a four-month-old puppy or kitten should eat a food high in calories, protein, and other nutrients specifically meant to encourage growth. Ounce for ounce, puppy or kitten food is higher in these than any other type of food is, save for perhaps a diet fed to pregnant or nursing mothers. If your six-year-old tabby ate kitten food instead of an adult formula, he would quickly gain weight.

Likewise, a dog or cat over seven or eight years old should probably not continue to eat the same food she ate as a three-year-old simply because, ounce for ounce, the young-adult food is higher in calories. That's why senior or "lite" pet foods were invented in the first place.

Feeding Multiple Pets Together, Unsupervised

Pets are like people in many ways, including appetite. Some dogs or cats simply eat more than others. You have all probably seen it: A hearty Labrador retriever inhales his food in twenty seconds, while a demure, dainty little Maltese takes an hour. A big, burly cat rescued from the street will eat quickly and greedily, whereas a quiet, stately Persian might take ages to finish. Status in the home also dictates who gets to eat what, and when. A dominant pet, if allowed to by the owner, will always eat the submissive pet's food if given the opportunity.

The mistake comes when owners try to feed pets like these at the same time, right next to each other. When that big happy retriever finishes his twenty-second meal, I can guarantee you he will do his darnedest to get his snout into the poor little Maltese's dish. When that is allowed to happen, the Lab eventually gains weight, while the Maltese starves. The same can happen with two cats of differing appetites and status.

The problem comes when this behavior goes relatively unnoticed by the owner, who might be busy preparing dinner or off in another part of the home. Without supervision, there is just no way to determine who is eating what.

The solution to this problem is simple. If you have multiple pets (even a dog and a cat), you must first observe them to see what their eating etiquette is. If you see one pet bullying another and eating her food, you will have to take action. The first thing you can try is placing the dishes at least five or six feet apart, and then watching to see what happens. Second, if one pet regularly finishes more quickly than the other, remove that pet when he is done so the other can finish in peace. If all else fails, feed the pets in separate rooms, and close the doors. Failing to try one of these options will ensure that the bully eventually becomes obese and the victim scrawny.

Feeding more than two pets at a time becomes a real challenge to your skills as a pet owner. In addition to trying the above-mentioned options, you may need to train the animals not to invade the other pets' privacy. You may even need to resort to multiple feeding times: one pet now, one pet in twenty minutes, and so on. Doing so will make it easier for you to mediate the situation.

If one of your pets seems to have a higher appetite than the others, consider feeding her at least two times per day, or perhaps even three. This will help satisfy her higher-than-normal food drive, so that she will be better able to control herself while feeding with the others.

Feeding Your Pet While Getting
Something from the Refrigerator

Dogs and cats are smart. They easily figure out just what the refrigerator is, and what it contains. So, when they hear the telltale suctioning sound of the refrigerator door being pulled open, they make a beeline for it. When you turn around with some leftovers in hand, who is sitting or standing there, so nice and pretty, gazing at you with adorable, yearning eyes? "Please sir, may I have some more?" they seem to say. And what do most of us do? We give in! "Here you go, boy! Have a slice of baloney!" We truly are suckers for this. Even I fall for it every now and then.

If your pet is fat, you must not fall for it. Do not allow yourself to be trained by your dog or cat. Simply refuse to give him anything. Ignore him. Within six to eight weeks, you should begin to see the manipulative begging at the refrigerator door go away. Let him know that the only time he will receive food from you or any other family member is at feeding time, or during a training period. Case closed.

Feeding Your Pet While Cooking

While some pets learn to beg at the refrigerator door, others master begging during food preparation. When you are preparing the family meal, the smell of food permeates the air. To a dog or cat, this can be intoxicating and very exciting. You might be cutting cheese for a sandwich or slicing meat for stew, and who appears by your side like magic but loyal Fido or Felix, looking as cute and needy as a Dickens street urchin. So what do you do? You surrender to your pet's pleas and give her a taste, and then another and another. After months of this, the behavior becomes ingrained in both of you, and the pet becomes fat.

Your overweight pet should not be the family's official taste tester. Avoid the pet's attempts to seduce you with that "look." Ignore her, or banish her from the kitchen while cooking. She must understand that her food comes from her dish, at feeding time.

Feeding Your Pet from the Dinner Table

Years ago I tried to help an elderly woman with a dominant, antisocial, aggressive, overweight Llhasa apso. The dog was a terror, biting visitors, mail carriers, and even members of the family. The dog completely ruled the poor woman's life, though I'm not so sure she didn't in some way actually like having such a demanding character to fuss over.

Part of my procedure is to go to the home and observe the dynamics as well as the conditions and physical layout. Seeing these firsthand can often help an animal behaviorist decide what course of action to take to correct the pet's bad behavior. Nine times out of ten, the behavior that needs correcting is that of the owner's. This case was a classic example.

Because I had worked with the dog for a week or so before the home visit, I was spared the humiliation of being bitten upon entering the home. Nonetheless, Muffin (yes, that was his name) wasn't all too thrilled with me being there. I asked Muffin's owner to just go about her daily activities without paying me any mind; I was just an observer staying for dinner.

When she set the dinner table, I immediately noticed something odd. Though she and I were the only ones eating, a third place was set on the table, with only a bowl, no silverware. The chair at that setting had a little footstool placed on it, its surface almost level with the tabletop. I saw what was coming but simply did not want to believe it.

Sure enough, as the owner and I sat down to roast chicken with mashed potatoes and gravy, so did Muffin. Perched atop his little footstool, he could easily put his muzzle into the bowl in front of him. The bowl was not a dog bowl; it was china, nicer than what I used myself at home.

As we ate, Muffin's owner periodically dished chicken, potatoes, and gravy into his bowl. He would of course gobble it down, then yip at her insistently until she doled more food into his bowl. I sat there, astonished at the scene, this little canine despot barking out dinner selections to his elderly submissive servant, who enjoyed the entire process immensely, as if Muffin were her son finally back from the Great War, psychologically scarred but physically whole.

This surreal feeding was of course in addition to Muffin's regular dinner, which he had eaten an hour before. Needless to say, the dog was obese, and I was dumbfounded. Try as I might, I could not get this woman to change her ways, and to see that it was she who had created this portly little dictator. After biting several more guests in the home (precipitating a lawsuit), the dog had to be put to sleep.

This of course is the most exaggerated example of improper feeding that I can report, but it certainly helps make a point. Allowing your pet to beg food from you at the dinner table will make him not only fat, but a behavioral nightmare as well. The poor woman had unknowingly created a dominant monster, in part by allowing him to dominate every aspect of the home, including dinnertime. She was his submissive servant, and he reveled in it.

If your cat or dog is overweight, all of her food *must* be fed to her *in her food dish*, at the scheduled feeding time. The only exception to this rule comes when small treats are being used for training purposes. If you allow begging to occur at the table, both you and the pet will quickly become addicted to the fun of it, eventually resulting in obesity for the pushy pet. (Note: For more on the role of food in training and in establishing leadership with your pet, see chapter 6.)

Feeding Your Pet Unwanted or Uneaten Food

Your pet is not a garbage disposal! If you have decided that some food item no longer meets human standards and should be thrown away, don't instead give it to your pet, in an attempt not to waste it. If you no longer deem the food edible, throw it out. Don't let your overweight pet be your leftover catchall.

Special Feeding Tips for the Cat Owner and Dog Owner

Though similar in many behavioral and physiological aspects, dogs and cats are also quite different in a number of areas, including dietary needs. Accordingly, I'd like to list some specific guidelines for each species, so that you might best serve your pet. By comparing and contrasting, you will be able to see where dog and cat needs coincide and where they differ.

A brief summary of a dog's dietary needs:

- needs about a third less protein than a cat
- more tolerant of cooked grains than a cat
- needs slightly less fat in his diet than a cat
- weight affected much more quickly by free-feeding than with a cat
- generally speaking, has a higher food drive than a cat, and is less finicky
- tolerates a dry-food diet better than a cat
- can exhibit more food-aggressive behavior than a cat
- can tolerate a lower water content in his food due to his willingness to drink water when needed
- can suffer from bloat
- pound for pound, needs fewer calories than a cat

A brief summary of a cat's dietary needs:

- needs about a third more protein and fat than a dog

- less tolerant of grain-based foods than a dog
- needs a higher percentage of water in her food than a dog due to a lower frequency of drinking, and to prevent the formation of stones in the bladder or kidneys
- lower food drive than a dog
- less tolerant of dry food than a dog
- generally less food aggressive than a dog
- less apt to gain weight on a free-feeding schedule than a dog
- not likely to suffer from bloat
- pound for pound, needs more calories than a dog

Breed-Specific Tips on Feeding

Generally the basic rules of feeding we've covered apply to all cats and dogs. Certain breeds do require some dietary "tweaking," however. As the number of cat and dog breeds currently existing are in the hundreds, each breed cannot be addressed here. However, some basic guidelines can be established for both cats and dogs. Dog breeds, being more varied in both appearance and size, often require distinctly different feeding patterns than do cats breeds, which on the whole have less variation in both size and behavior.

Dog Breed Feeding Variations

Generally, the larger the breed, the fewer calories per pound should be fed. Hunting, herding, or sled-pulling dogs, purposely bred to be more active, will require more calories per day than less active dogs. Large breeds, due to their vulnerability to bloat, need their daily food rations split into smaller, more frequent meals. Dog breeds kept in colder climates will need to eat more calories per day than those kept in more temperate environments. Sight hounds such as greyhounds, salukis, or whippets generally have more finicky appetites than other breeds. Some toy breeds such as the Maltese, Chihuahua, toy spaniel, or papillon will also be more finicky than more active and gregarious breeds such as Rottweilers, German shepherds, or Labrador retrievers.

Cat Breed Feeding Variations

The same weight rules apply: Generally, the larger the cat, the fewer calories per pound body weight needed. This rule becomes negligible with most cats, however, because the variation in weights according to breed is much smaller. The larger breeds, such as the Norwegian forest cat, could weigh over twenty pounds, whereas a smaller breed such as a Cornish rex might weigh less than half that. (Variations in dog breed sizes are much more profound: A Chihuahua might weigh four pounds, whereas a Saint Bernard could weigh in at over two hundred, fifty times as heavy!) Cat breeds such as the Burmese or Siamese are much more active than a breed such as the Persian and must therefore take in more calories per pound body weight.

Cats spending lots of time outdoors need more calories than those kept indoors. Cats kept in colder climates, especially if they often venture outdoors, need more calories per day than those in more temperate climates.

Nutritional Supplements that Can Aid in Pet Weight Loss and Promote Good Health

Any obese pet can benefit from having the fiber content of his diet increased by 5 to 15 percent. This can be done by adding whole cooked grains such as brown rice, oats, or barley, or by adding some type of cooked vegetable such as broccoli, green beans, or Brussels sprouts. For cats, replace only 5 percent of her normal food with fibrous materials. Dogs can go as high as 15 percent. Adding garlic will also raise the fiber levels while providing beneficial vitamins, minerals, and antioxidants. Replacing sixty or seventy calories of the pet's food with one whole raw egg will provide protein, necessary fatty acids, and lecithin, a nutrient beneficial to liver function. Also adding a small amount of acidophilus yogurt to the pet's diet each day will help renew beneficial bacteria in the intestines, necessary to proper digestion.

Fasting

Wild dogs and cats regularly go through periods of involuntary fasting, a natural process that helps keep them motivated and healthy. Periods of fasting also help clear the gastrointestinal tract of toxins and waste materials.

Your pet can benefit from a one- or two-day light fast each month. It won't hurt his health at all and will help restore the food drive in a pet who has become finicky. It will also help the obese pet lose a bit more weight than would normally be possible. For the first fast, try feeding your pet only a half cup of brown rice cooked in chicken broth once each day for two days straight. Provide plenty of water as well. The pet's digestive tract will be rested and cleansed, and weight will be lost. If the pet exhibits no profound behavioral or physiological reactions to this method, try going to a water-only fast the next month. Do it for one day only. You will find that trying this with your dog or cat once per month will improve his digestion and elimination habits.

Vary the Diet

Dogs and cats in the wild generally eat a very predictable diet. Wolves, for example, collectively take down deer or elk—prey animals that are as large or larger than themselves—and consume the entire animal, including the bones and stomach contents. They will of course eat smaller prey if necessary; many an unfortunate hare falls victim to hungry, appreciative wolves. Wild cats also prey on large creatures, but, due to their more solitary hunting practices, they cannot always kill larger prey and need to settle for smaller animals from time to time.

Nevertheless, both canines and felines in the wild have one thing in common: They eat meat, and lots of it. Their diets are not nearly as varied as ours. As omnivores, our digestive tracts can tolerate a wider variety of foods than can the simpler systems of dogs or cats. Dogs and cats in the wild do eat plant material, however, mostly as a consequence of consuming the prey's stomach and the partially digested foods within. So, though much more predictable than our own diet, dogs and cats in the wild do have some dietary variation occurring.

In contrast, domestic dogs and cats rarely have any variety. Most owners feed them the exact same food day in and day out. Though nutritionally acceptable, feeding your dog or cat the same thing every day has a few disadvantages. First, pets fed the same diet every day for years can easily become sick when given a new type of food. Most owners know that switching a pet from one food to another usually needs to be done gradually, over a two- or three-week period, to avoid stomach upset, diarrhea, and possible allergic reactions to the new food.

Second, eating the exact same thing can be just plain boring. Remember, these are intelligent creatures, not goldfish. And, as stated before, a bored pet tends to sleep more (lowering her overall metabolism) and eat more (to alleviate her boredom). Both these behaviors eventually result in weight gain.

Adding some variation to your dog or cat's diet will:

- help his digestive system better cope with slight changes in diet
- help reduce possible allergic reactions to new foods
- assure that your pet is getting complete nutrition
- make the eating experience more exciting
- relieve boredom, resulting in less lethargy and a resulting decrease in sleep time, which raises metabolism and helps burn calories
- reduce amounts eaten as a result of less boredom

Add variation to your pet's diet very slowly. Stick with her normal food, but decrease the amount slightly and add other nutritious foods to it. For example, if your dog eats only dry food, mix in a little canned food. Or, if your cat eats only canned, mix in some high-quality dry food. Also try adding items like raw ground meat, a whole raw egg, cooked vegetables, or cooked whole grains. Just make sure that you add just a small amount each time, and that the total number of calories does not exceed the number you have calculated the pet needs to gradually lose weight. Vary what you add slightly each day so that your pet won't know what great new taste is coming. You will find your cat or dog more excited, responsive, healthier, and happier because of it. The resulting anticipation and response will slightly raise her metabolic rate, helping the weight loss process along.

How to Decide on a Feeding Option Best Suited to Your Overweight Pet

Nothing is written in stone. If you are feeding your cat or dog a certain type and amount of food each day and he still seems to be gaining weight, check the number of calories the pet is taking in each day, and adjust the amount accordingly. Your pet might need fewer calories per day than another pet of the same age and size; it's all trial and error. Or alter the type of food, the frequency of feeding, or the time of feeding. Often when or what a pet eats can be as important as how much she eats. The telling factor will always be what your pet weighs at the end of each week. Never forget to check this. It is the best litmus test for success or failure.

If dietary adjustments do not seem to help your cat or dog lose unwanted weight, read on. Chapter 4, "Exercise," may be the answer. Adjusting an overweight pet's caloric intake is vital, but so is increasing his caloric expenditures. Chapter 4 will help you do this.

4. Exercise

The Overlooked Key to Your Pet's Weight Loss

Second in importance only to diet, the level of daily activity in which a dog or cat participates will to a large degree determine her caloric expenditures. Lethargic homebound pets, denied the chance to be active on a regular basis, will almost always gradually put on weight. By their fifth or sixth year of life, most of these pets are overweight. This chapter will explain the vital importance of daily exercise for your pet, and will aid you in choosing exercises most appropriate to her unique lifestyle. Beneficial exercises for dogs *and* cats are included, as are activities that might not be appropriate for certain types of pets.

Let me again ask the question: Why don't wild dogs and cats get fat? Answer: Because they don't have the time! They spend their entire lives expending great amounts of energy trying to survive. Hunting, defending, reproducing, and fending off the elements burn incredible amounts of energy, requiring in response a hearty appetite. Wild African dogs, for example, will often run for hours across the savannah in an attempt to track and kill prey. Cheetahs, the world's fastest land animal, will sprint upward of seventy miles per hour, day after day, in pursuit of elusive prey. These animals are long, lean, calorie-burning machines, nature's perfect engines.

In comparison, your jolly old basset hound or Persian cat doesn't exactly rip up the African turf in search of his next meal. More likely he wakes up from a warm nap and sleepily meanders over to his trusty food dish; this is his equivalent of the "great hunt." *Brave hunter slays bowl of kibble.* Needless to say, this type of "hunt" doesn't burn many calories. But, as we mentioned, the domestic cat or dog's food drive remains nearly as strong as his wild brethren's, setting him up for eventual weight gain.

The problem is compounded by owners, who often do not have the time to exercise their pets, or who simply think their furry friends don't need it, that they are animals and thus have naturally high metabolisms. Wrong! Dogs and cats today, especially those kept in urban settings, often get less exercise than many of their owners, who, in addition to working eight to ten hours per day, work out at the gym, jog, cycle, or play sports. When was the last time your dog or cat had such an active day?

Exercise, for pets and humans alike, is a vital ingredient in any weight loss program. In addition to burning calories outright, it raises the metabolic thermostat of the body, allowing your pet to burn more calories at rest than she otherwise would. Exercise builds muscle as well, and because muscles are calorie "engines," developing your pet's muscles will help burn more calories. In addition, exercise has a profoundly positive effect on mood and attitude. During strenuous activity, the endocrine systems of dogs and cats, like humans, produce *endorphins,* naturally occurring hormones that help create a positive, alert, almost euphoric mind-set.

People or pets who exercise on a regular basis become more confident, happy, and psychologically sound than those who never lift a finger. Therapists who work with persons suffering from depression almost always prescribe exercise to their patients for this reason. It stands to reason, then, that exercise should be a mandatory component of any pet weight loss regimen.

When discussing exercise for pets, most people assume it only applies to dogs, and that cats are simply too independent and headstrong to participate in any type of exercise program designed by a mere human. Dogs, people think, are much more cooperative and easy to motivate into running, playing, chasing, or fetching games. Though it is true that dogs, being pack oriented, hierarchical creatures, respond more readily to commands, training, or group-related events, cats can be taught to participate in a variety of strenuous physical activities without too much trouble. Though the list of possible cat exercises is limited in comparison to those for canines, numerous effective activities can be taught to almost any cat, if the owner takes the time to do so.

This section will provide you with a wide variety of exercises you can encourage your pet to perform, be he cat or dog. Some will require more time input on your part than others, whereas many will be initiated and sustained by your pet with little investment from you. Most of the recommended exercises will have one thing in common: They will be fueled by the pet's instinctive drives, particularly the predatory and social drives. You won't have to twist your pet's arm, but only provide him with the right stimuli and the right motivation. Many of the exercises here will be very familiar to you, while others won't, especially those for cats. Try the ones you think your pet will respond most readily to; you know your pet best, and you will know what he will be willing to do. Just make sure you allow the pet to participate in some form of aerobic activity every day of his life, to keep his metabolism cooking along and to promote overall good health.

Exercise Dos and Don'ts: Basic Guidelines

Before you begin exercising your cat or dog, there are a few safety and behavioral guidelines you should follow to ensure your pet's physical and psychological safety. Remember that a dog or cat has the reasoning capacity of a two-year-old child and can become worried or afraid if asked to do something he has never done before. For example, taking a four-month-old puppy to a dog park crowded with many large adult dogs can be frightening and potentially damaging to the little youngster. Rather than overwhelming him, it's a better idea to introduce the puppy to groups of strange adult dogs more slowly, particularly if he is a little on the shy side. Start with the neighbor's dog, or go to the dog park at a time when the crowds are thin. Or, attempt to involve the pup with dogs closer to his own age, at a puppy-training class, for instance.

Never force a pet to do anything she doesn't want to do. Exercise and activity has to be fun for the pet; if she feels any fear or hesitation about performing some new behavior, then back off. Either try it again in quieter surroundings or find a less threatening exercise. What a gregarious Lab is willing to do might be an overwhelming task for a more shy, demure saluki. What a sociable Siamese will happily endure might be too challenging for a Cornish rex or a Persian. Use your best judgment, and err on the side of caution.

Never force an adult cat to socialize with unfamiliar

cats, and *never* put him in among strange dogs. Only involve your cat with pets he knows and likes; remember, cats don't socialize as readily as dogs do and could easily become terrified or aggressive. Though dogs and cats can often get along well, realize that they are by nature quite apprehensive toward each other. And also know that most dogs will, if given the chance, be very predatory toward all but the most confident cats.

Never force a cat or dog to exercise beyond her potential. If a pet is obese, avoid highly strenuous activities such as jogging long distances, long swims, fetch sessions that go on too long, or any level of exercise that could damage her musculoskeletal or cardiovascular systems. Avoid exercises that involve an obese cat or dog jumping up or down from high places, as the resulting impacts could seriously damage the pet's back, legs, shoulders, or hips, due to the extra weight. Try jumping off of a chair while piggybacking a friend and you'll know what I mean.

Don't exercise your pet right after his dinner. Blood in the pet's body is diverted to the digestive process at this time, making vigorous exercise difficult. And in large dogs, of course, exercise right after eating can bring on bloat, which is often fatal. Wait at least one hour before vigorously exercising your pet.

Some dogs, notably retrievers, will exercise, play, or fetch literally until their hearts give out. A function of their breed-specific profile is that sometimes they just won't quit. Though admirable, letting this occur with an obese retriever isn't a good idea. Know when to stop the exercise; do not let your obese dog's willingness to go on and on trick you into letting her. She could severely hurt herself. As the pet loses weight, you can increase the time of the play sessions, but in the meantime, know when to say "that's enough." With an obese dog, it is a good idea to limit exercise sessions (excluding walks, which do not put much stress on the pet) to ten or fifteen minutes to start, to ensure her cardiovascular system is not overloaded. Likewise, when exercising an obese cat, make sure to limit sessions to ten or fifteen minutes.

Exercises for Dogs

Due to the canine's sociability and willingness to please, getting one to participate in some form of exercise isn't at all difficult. If you own one, you probably know this, and are already aware of a number of activities your pooch loves to perform. Some dogs are less motivated than others, however; breeds like the Maltese, Pekingese, or Clumber spaniel might not be as eager to participate as would a retriever, shepherd, pointer, or terrier. Nevertheless, there should be an exercise for every dog here; as with everything, it's just a matter of trial and error on your part. When you find one your dog likes, stick with it. Make an attempt to find an activity that your dog will readily participate in without you having to bribe him with treats, as this will only negate the advantages of the exercise. Use the sheer pleasure the dog experiences as reinforcement, and throw in lots and lots of physical and verbal praise, often just as effective as a treat. Your pooch will soon look forward to his daily workout, if he doesn't from the start.

Fetch

Probably *the classic* dog exercise, fetch is also one of the best all-around activities for your dog, for a number of reasons. First, it is often an easy exercise to encourage and maintain, as most dogs have an instinctive desire to chase after small, fast-moving objects. Because it's an expression of the predatory instinct, it's not hard to get a dog to run after, pick up, and bring back an object she covets.

For those who already have dogs who love to fetch, this is a no-brainer. Just take the pooch to a fenced-in, relatively distraction-free area and have at it. Whether you use a ball, Frisbee, stick, rubber toy, or stuffed animal doesn't matter. Just encourage the dog at first; get him stoked, then give the object a toss. One piece of advice: Always quit when the dog is still excited and in fetch mode. Don't wait until the pet becomes bored with the activity, because this can begin to erode his desire and love for the exercise. Ten minutes is plenty of time for a session. Try to repeat this at least two or three times each day, to get a good number of calories burned. Numerous short, intense, fun sessions are much more motivating and fun for the dog than one hour-long, never-ending marathon. Never work fetch for so long the dog loses interest and walks away.

Initiating fetch with dogs not familiar with it is not hard. Though you should ideally start out with a puppy, adolescent or adult dogs can learn it just fine. The first step is to find some object that your dog seems to really like. It can be anything, provided it's not small enough to swallow, and it has no pieces that the dog can rip off and choke on, such as stuffed toys with buttons or floppy ears hanging off. Also, it's a good idea to only bring the object out and into your dog's presence when you plan to play fetch. This will keep your dog's interest high; if you leave the object out in plain sight all the time, it will cease to be irresistible to the pet. Why should he chase something that is always available? Realize that for most dogs it's the *object* they covet, and not necessarily the chasing of it.

At first, simply bring the object out and let your dog see it, preferably inside the home, with no distractions. Then make a very big deal over it; make it seem to the dog that this object is the best thing since sirloin. If your dog sees you, the leader, coveting something, chances are he will too. Toss it around and retrieve it yourself. Tease the dog with it and then hide it under your arm. Throw it up in the air and catch it. Soon your dog will begin to really *want* that thing you have. If it's a tennis ball, try cutting a small slit in it and slipping a few treats inside; the scent will really get your dog worked up. The idea is to make this thing irresistible to your pet. Give your dog a treat or two whenever he sees or touches the object.

Then put it away. The dog will think, "Gee, you got me all excited, and now it's gone. Bring that thing back here!" Wait a few hours and then repeat the teasing session, this time tossing the object a few feet and praising your dog whenever he shows any inclination to chase after it. If he chases it and picks it up in his mouth, quickly praise him, get down low, and call him to you. If and when he comes with the object, praise him lavishly! At first you can give him a treat or two, not only as a reward, but as a way to get the dog to release the toy so you can toss it again.

Keep working this in the home, gradually lengthening the distance you throw the toy. And remember not to work your dog too long; at this stage, quit after he fetches the toy three or four times. Try to repeat the sessions every few hours, and really be encouraging! Make a big deal about it so the dog can see you, the leader, involved and excited. That will ensure his desire to participate.

Eventually you should move outdoors with the training. Start in a backyard where there are few or no distractions to interrupt the dog's concentration. Then, very gradually, over a period of weeks, introduce some distractions, such as a friend sitting on the lawn reading a book, a radio playing, or a flag flapping in the breeze. The objective is to get your dog to fixate on the fetching and nothing else. If you don't teach your dog to focus on the toy, you won't be able to achieve a sustained fetch at the park, or in an area where other people or dogs are playing.

Again, work this exercise for short periods, to keep the dog's interest level up. Stop when he's still motivated, put the toy away, then repeat a few hours later. Eventually you will have a calorie-burning, fun exercise for your overweight dog to perform whenever you feel he needs exercise.

The Recall or "Come"

Essential to keeping a dog safe and out of trouble, the recall or "come" command can also be used to exercise your dog. Properly taught, the recall will have your dog running to you over short, medium, or long distances, effectively burning lots of calories and improving cardiovascular function.

The first step is of course to teach your dog to come to you reliably, if she doesn't already. Ideally you should start when the dog is just a puppy. While in the home, place yourself four feet away from the pooch, crouch down low, and call the dog to you, being as encouraging and happy as possible. Actually use the dog's name, followed by a sweet-sounding, lively "Come here!" Make it sound happy and inviting. Do not make your "come" command sound threatening or angry, and never call your dog over to you and then punish her. Doing so is the surest way to teach her *not* to come. Young pups will almost always come to you when given a happy invitation. When she does come over, pet her lavishly and give her a small treat. Then wait a minute or so, until the pup becomes distracted by something or someone else in the room. When she is not paying any attention to you at all, repeat the inviting request to the dog, rewarding her with praise and a small treat once she is frolicking all over you. Keep working this indoors, gradually increasing the distance until you can get the dog to come to you from anywhere in the home. This method, by the way, will work for adult dogs as well, but it works better with impressionable youngsters.

Once you have a reliable recall inside, switch to a quiet backyard. Clip a six-foot leash onto the dog's collar, to guarantee that the pet will come to you. The trick to getting a reliable recall under any circumstances is to ensure that the dog *has no other option but to come*. Work the command in the same manner, realizing that the dog may not want to come to you at first, due to all of the distractions outside. To encourage the dog, try backing away from her quickly, while holding onto the leash. *As soon as the dog begins coming to you*, praise her. That is a crucial step: If you wait until the dog is in your lap, you've waited too long. Then give her a small treat. Continue to praise the dog for coming to you, but begin giving her a treat every other time. Remember, the trick is to eventually get the dog to come *to you and your praise*, not the treat.

Once the dog is coming to you reliably on the six-foot leash, switch to a longer line, one that is at least fifteen or twenty feet long. A retractable leash or even a length of clothesline will do. Take the dog out into the yard and let her get distracted by a smell or a sound. Then, crouch down and call her to you enthusiastically. If she does not come, give her a gentle pop with the long lead while saying "no"; then repeat the command to come. If necessary, actually start the dog toward you with the line. As soon as the pooch begins to come in your direction, praise her and be extremely enthusiastic. Clap, call her name, crouch down low, or do anything necessary to get her attention. Make yourself an irresistible target. When she does come, praise her and give her a treat.

Continue working this long-line recall as you introduce more and more distractions. Have two children play catch or a group of adults talk. The idea is to get the dog to respond no matter what happens to be going on. The line will ensure the dog never has the option of not coming; you can literally reel her in if necessary. If the dog learns that she can selectively ignore your command to come, you will never get a reliable recall.

Once you have the dog reliably coming to you in the yard on the long line, with distractions, it's time to take off the line and work her. For this, remove all distractions; let it just be you, the dog, and the scents of the backyard. Start this off-leash training from only five or six feet away, and reward the dog with a special treat when she comes to you. Gradually, over a period of days, lengthen the distance and continue rewarding with a treat and praise. Do not work the recall for more than a few minutes at a time, as the dog may get bored and decide to ignore you. Always quit when the dog is still psyched to come. Eventually the dog will see this off-leash recall as a game she likes to play. When you get to that stage, you're home free.

The last stage is of course to work the dog out at a large park. Use the long line first to ensure that the dog will come. Use some especially great treats, such as thin slices of hotdog or bits of ground beef, just to make certain the dog is paying attention. Once the long-line recall is working, try a few off-leash recalls in the park, from twenty or thirty feet away. After two or three off-leash successes, praise the dog and go home. Repeat it often, eventually getting the dog to come to you under any circumstance. Remember also to gradually wean her off treats and onto praise only.

Once you have taught your dog to come to you over a long distance, you can take her to the park, place her in a sit position, walk forty or fifty feet away, and call her to you enthusiastically. Your pet will sprint over to you in anticipation of your praise. Repeating this for ten or fifteen minutes will exercise your dog and burn lots of calories, helping with the weight loss.

For an even better workout, take a friend with you. Have the friend hold the dog while you run away at least fifty or sixty yards. Then have the friend release the dog while you simultaneously call her. Try clapping your hands as well, and getting down low, or even running away from the dog. Your pet will sprint to you as fast as she can; when she gets to you, praise her to no end. Then, have your friend do the same thing while you hold the dog. In effect, you will be bouncing the dog back and forth between you. She will have fun and get a terrific workout.

The "Round-Robin" Recall

Similar to the standard recall, this exercise involves having three or four people, arranged in a triad or square, each calling the dog to them in succession. After the dog has come to one person, another person immediately calls the dog, and this continues from person to person, with occasional treats given as rewards. The dog will see it as a fun game, and when done correctly, it will really burn calories and reinforce the recall command. The group can spread out as far as space will allow, making it a real aerobic challenge for the pet.

Jogging

Jogging with your dog can be an excellent way to get both of you in shape. In as few as fifteen or twenty minutes each day, your dog will really begin to show results quickly.

A few precautions need to be taken, however, before you begin this activity. First, make sure your dog is capable of doing it. Do not take a thirteen-year-old arthritic animal for daily runs, as he will suffer more than benefit. Do not take a severely obese dog jogging, as she may suffer cardiac or respiratory arrest while doing so. If your dog is more than 25 percent over her ideal weight, consider walking with her for twenty minutes instead, until her weight gets down low enough to make the activity safe. Also, do not take a small dog jogging for long distances, or at speeds so fast he can't keep up. Taking a Pomeranian or a Chihuahua for a three-mile jog at seven minutes per mile would be unforgivable. Use your common sense. If in doubt, take the smaller dog for a quick walk instead.

Make sure conditions are suitable for the activity. For instance, no dog should be required to go jogging in ninety- to one-hundred-degree heat. Temperatures below freezing should be avoided also, particularly for small dogs or for breeds with shorter coats, such as the greyhound or the pointer. Huskies, Malamutes, Samoyeds, and other arctic breeds should never be taken jogging when the temperature is over eighty degrees.

Before going jogging with your dog, make sure both of you have plenty of water. Upon returning, provide your dog (and yourself) with as much water as needed. Keeping prop-erly hydrated will prevent heat exhaustion for you both.

Lastly, don't take a dog jogging if she has any kind of

structural problems such as bad hips, shoulders, knees, or back. If any type of medical problem exists, talk to your veterinarian before beginning any type of jogging activity with your dog.

Walking

The time-honored dog exercise, taking your dog for a few walks each day can help him lose weight and relieve the boredom of being alone all day. Just getting out of his immediate surroundings and into a new area filled with different scents and sights can really perk up a lethargic, overweight dog's metabolism and spirit.

Find the time to take your dog for at least two (and preferably three) walks each day, of at least fifteen minutes in length. Try to make them brisk walks; get your dog's heart and lungs working (not to mention yours). Consider walking in new neighborhoods every so often, just for the change. Drive to a nice, wooded area and explore the place together. Look for some challenges too; walk up a steep hill, then down it. Scramble up a grassy ridge, or race the last one hundred feet together. You won't win, but you'll have fun anyway.

Walking (over jogging) is recommended for dogs with structural or medical problems, geriatric dogs, and dogs who are significantly obese. Also, walk, don't run, if it is hot out. If you have two or more dogs, consider walking them instead of jogging, as they might get all tangled up, resulting in a spill for all of you.

Make sure to use a strong leash of at least five feet in length (though six feet would be better). Having your dog trained not to pull on the leash will also help make the walk a bit more pleasant for you. Avoid walking in heavily trafficked roads and areas with many bikers or joggers.

Biking

If your dog is in excellent aerobic health, no more than a few pounds overweight, and large enough to keep up, you might consider riding your bike with your dog running beside you. This can be a tricky exercise to perform safely, however. The dog can get part of her body caught in the spokes or the gears of the bike. Also, other bikes on the bike path can pose a threat. Additionally, cars on the street can threaten both you and your dog. Your dog has to be very responsive to you and your position, and must slow and stop exactly when you do.

Start out slowly, in an area with no traffic or distractions. Consider having your dog run on the right side of your bike, as running on the left will expose her to oncoming bikes, joggers, or cars. Keep to the right of the street or path, and don't interfere with others who might want to go faster. Consider attaching your dog's leash to a two- or three-foot-long wooden pole lashed to the handlebars, seat, or frame; doing so will prevent the leash from getting caught in the spokes or gears. Don't try this with more than one dog; it's just too risky and complicated. But remember, your dog should be big enough and fit enough to keep up. Making a twelve-year-old bulldog run beside you at fifteen miles per hour would be unfair and cruel, so don't try it.

As with jogging, make sure you both drink water before and after biking. And do not make your dog run more than a few miles at a time, even if she is in great shape. The cumulative stress of running all those miles day in and day out can have deleterious effects on your dog's musculoskeletal system. If unsure of your dog's ability to keep up, consult your veterinarian.

Hiking

As with walking or jogging, hiking with your dog can be a great calorie-burning activity. Usually not possible on a daily basis due to people's work schedules, hiking is often done on weekends, perhaps at most once per week. For that reason, try not to push your dog too hard with this one, especially if he is overweight, old, small, or prone to any musculoskeletal problems.

First, choose an area that permits dogs on the trails. Many local, state, and national parks do not allow pets on the trails, so check first. Second, make sure you take a leash with you, as most dog-friendly trails do require the pet to be on a leash. If the trail does not require this, only take your dog if he is not in any way aggressive to persons or other animals, and if he can relieve himself in the proper areas, and not on the trail itself.

Start out with a short trail and make sure to take enough water for both of you. Pet shops now sell small pet vests that contain removable water bottles; purchasing one can lighten your load and give your pet an additional workout. Be sure not to overtax your dog, especially if he is not used to this level of exercise. Old, small, injured, or sick pets should never be forced to hike, as it could cause serious injury or illness. Again, consult your veterinarian if you're unsure whether hiking would be right for your pet.

Swimming

Though not all dogs like to swim, most, if not all, know how to, even those who have never been given the opportunity. Some, notably retrievers, Newfoundlands, and spaniels love the water and will dive in without hesitation. If your dog takes a liking to the water, by all means bring her down to an appropriate body of water and let her swim to her heart's content. Retrieving a stick, ball, or some other floating object will give the dog a goal while in the water. In the meantime she will get an excellent aerobic workout.

There are a number of precautions to take, however, before letting your dog swim. First, the body of water must be safe. Any pond, lake, river, or ocean that is polluted should be off-limits to your dog. Second, fast-moving rivers or streams or active surf should be avoided, especially by owners of small or old dogs, as they might get swept away. Third, avoid any bodies of water containing creatures that could hurt or kill your pet. Infectious protozoa, bacteria, snakes, alligators, and even sharks have been known to harm or even kill swimming dogs, so beware. If in doubt, check with the local authorities or the county health department.

Don't let your dog swim in a reservoir used by the public for drinking water. Also, prevent your dog from relieving herself anywhere near any body of water; make sure she is at least one hundred feet away, and, whenever possible, remove feces in a plastic bag and discard in an appropriate place.

Dogs who swim every day can run the risk of getting dry skin and a dry coat, not so much from the water itself but from the increased number of baths needed to get the dog clean again. You will need to bathe a dog who swims much more often, so consider buying a shampoo and conditioner that is very gentle. If in doubt, consult your veterinarian, who will be able to recommend good products, and who will also be able to spot any type of unusual skin irritations that may pop up due to the effects of the frequent swims. In general, groom the canine swimmer on a daily basis; remove matted hair and keep it combed out to prevent impossible tangles, which can only be removed by a professional groomer.

As with any exercise, start your dog out slowly and don't overdo it. Be aware that a small dog's body temperature lowers much more quickly than a larger pet's, so don't let a small dog swim as long. Even a larger dog will chill quickly if the water is cold enough, so avoid extremely cold bodies of water if possible, unless the dog is simply running in and out of the water without really swimming. Thinner dogs such as whippets, greyhounds, or salukis will chill much faster than beefier breeds, so be aware of that as well. In addition, some heavily muscled dogs such as rottweilers or pit bulls are much denser and less buoyant than other breeds, so keep your eye out for them tiring, especially in fast-moving water.

Swimming can be an excellent exercise for dogs with any type of musculoskeletal problems because their bodies are virtually weightless while in the water. Choose short swims over jogging for any dog with hip, back, shoulder, or knee problems.

In addition to shampooing and conditioning the coat of a canine swimmer, you will need to clean out such a dog's ears more often, as the water will promote extra wax buildup. Consult your veterinarian for the best method or have him or her do it for you. The dog's eyes may become red or inflamed from time to time as well, so keep a close watch, and restrict swim time if this occurs.

Overall, swimming is an excellent exercise for most dogs and will help burn off those unwanted canine calories quickly. With the proper precautions, a swim or two each week will put your overweight dog back on the road to good health.

Hide-and-Seek

There probably isn't a dog alive who hasn't at some point played and enjoyed a good game of hide-and-seek with his owner. Usually a game owners play with their puppies, this fun activity can be played with adult dogs as well with no real training. Chances are you won't be able to fool your dog for very long because his nose and speed will give him a distinct advantage. No matter; hide-and-seek will be a great exercise for your dog, as well as a good bonding experience.

You might do well to have a friend help you with this one at first. After playing with your dog for a minute or so, have your friend hold on to the dog while you disappear into another room. Instruct your friend to wait a few moments, then let the dog go and say, "Go find him [or her]!" Some dogs might need a little encouragement, but most will instinctively seek out their hidden masters. Once the dog does find you hiding behind a door or underneath a stairwell, praise him lavishly and give him a small treat. Then repeat the exercise. Eventually you won't need the help of your friend; the dog will begin to anticipate the "rules" and give you enough time to hide. You can even tell him to "wait" while you go hide, and then call out to him from your hiding spot. Use your imagination when designing the intricacies of the game. Take the fun outside into the yard or a park, or play it at a friend's home, where your dog might have to work a bit harder to find you. Just make sure he gets plenty of exercise in the process. Do use small treats at first, but slowly replace them with physical and verbal praise over a few weeks' time.

Agility Competition

Canine agility clubs exist in most areas of the United States and Europe. Dedicated to developing and improving coordination, dexterity, and overall physical agility, these clubs teach dogs to jump over obstacles, go through tunnels, weave through poles, balance on a teeter-totter, leap over abysses, and do all manner of spectacular stunts. In addition to providing great physical challenge, these clubs teach the participating dogs how to be confident and competitive and how to interact with other dogs and persons on a friendly, cooperative basis. You can probably find an agility club close to you by calling a local canine-training facility, the local humane society, or your veterinarian. If your dog likes to be physical and tolerates the presence of other dogs, you shouldn't have a problem enrolling her.

Breeds such as the Border collie, Australian shepherd, Jack Russell terrier, vizsla, or fox terrier do exceptionally well at agility, but just about any dog will get the hang of it. Medium-sized, athletically inclined dogs do the best, as they tend to be nimble, fast, and big enough to handle the high jumps. Very large, heavy dogs can do well also, but they might have trouble with sprains or pulls due to the constant jumping and leaping. Small breeds, though they have lots of fun, might not be able to get over the higher or wider jumps.

Over several weeks your dog will learn how to jump over things, go through things (such as a plastic tunnel), weave through closely spaced poles, and go up and down steeply inclined ramps. Eventually strung together, these challenges become one long obstacle course that your dog runs for time. Your pet will have a blast and burn lots of calories in the process.

You can set up your own miniature obstacle course at home, in the yard or inside if need be. Start with setting a yardstick atop two piles of books about eight inches high, two or three feet apart. Have your dog sit or stand on one side of the yardstick and position yourself on the other. Then, with a treat in hand, enthusiastically encourage the dog to jump over the yardstick to your side to get the small treat that awaits. Try reaching over the yardstick at first with the treat, and actually tempt the dog over; otherwise he might just decide to go around instead. Work on this for a few days, eventually getting the pooch to do it on his own. Then, increase the height of the jump until the dog is sailing over the two- or three-foot-high jump.

Try making a tunnel out of an old blanket or shower curtain suspended over a row of chairs. Or go to the pet shop and buy a tunnel; they look like giant spring toys covered with plastic or fabric. These are very adaptable in that they can be stretched or contracted, varying the length according to the dog's confidence level. At first, simply encourage the dog to go in the tunnel after a treat. Then have a friend hold the dog at one end while you sit at the other end with a treat and encourage the dog through. At first you may have to climb halfway in and tempt the dog through, but eventually he will get the idea. Soon you will have your pooch rushing through the tunnel, wondering what fun thing will be at the other end.

You can set up a weave course by placing four or five chairs in a row, two or three feet apart. Then, with the dog sitting at one end, tempt him through the chairs with a treat beneath his nose. Encourage him to weave through the chairs, and then reward him with the treat. You can also buy agility weave poles at a well-stocked pet shop.

Eventually you should connect all of the obstacles and teach your dog to run the entire course as fast as he can. He will have enormous amounts of fun, burn hundreds of calories, and get a tremendous confidence boost. Just make sure your pet is in adequate condition before trying the jumps, as they can be very hard on an obese dog's joints. Also, if your dog is over eight or nine years old, consider keeping the jump height at under eighteen inches.

Stair Climbing

A great exercise for your dog to do indoors on a rainy or inclement day is simply running up and down a flight of stairs. Available to urban, suburban, and rural dwellers alike, stairs can provide (as most of us know) a great way to get the heart and lungs working. Calories are burned, and aerobic fitness is improved.

Most dogs can participate in this exercise, though the very smallest toy breeds might have some trouble getting momentum. Even getting these dogs to climb five or six steps as rapidly as possible will serve the purpose, however. Dogs who are seriously obese may have some trouble, as might geriatric pets over ten or twelve years of age. If you have a dog in one of these categories, make sure not to overwork her, since this, as with every exercise, could lead to serious medical problems.

Begin the exercise with the help of a friend if you can. Have him or her hold on to your dog's collar at the bottom of a flight of stairs, while you position yourself at the top. Then, as you enthusiastically call your dog, have your friend let go of the collar. Odds are your dog will bolt up the steps to you. As soon as the dog begins coming up, praise her verbally. Then, when she gets to you, give her a coveted treat, perhaps a small bit of cheese, and physically praise her. Then have your friend call the dog down to him or her, praising the pet in the same fashion as soon as she begins descending. When the dog arrives at the bottom, your friend should also reward her with a treat and with physical praise. Continue ping-ponging the dog in this fashion, gradually using fewer treats and more physical praise, until treats are used only once or twice per session.

You can expand this exercise to include more than one flight of stairs, or to include the stairs as part of a larger obstacle course. When playing hide-and-seek (as described earlier), make sure to hide on a different level of the home, so the dog must climb or descend stairs to find you. If your dog knows the recall or "come" command well, you can randomly disappear upstairs and then call the pooch to you. She will come running, right up those steep, calorie-burning stairs. Having your dog rapidly climb five or six flights of stairs each day will take barely any time at all, and will help her lose weight or stay trim. (Note: If your dog has any history of heart or respiratory disease, or suffers from any type of joint disorder, consult your veterinarian before attempting this exercise.)

Playing at a Dog Park

Few exercises can burn up as many doggy calories as a prolonged period of play at a regulated, enclosed dog park. Available in many urban and suburban communities, these enclosed, well-maintained play areas not only let your dog unleash all his pent-up energies, but also allow him to enter into a complex canine social venue similar to that of his wild brethren. Watching your dog interact with ten or twenty others of his kind will be eye-opening. Behaviors you never thought your dog capable of will be openly expressed. He will try to dominate other dogs with body posturing, while discovering (with dismay) that more dominant dogs than him actually do exist. Though some ritualistic aggression may occur in the form of snarling or the baring of fangs, rarely will there be a full-blown dogfight. Some dogs, particularly ones who have had very little socialization, may be somewhat frightened at first and could show it by raising hackles (hair on the upper back), staying close to you, or running away from any kind of interaction. It is usually best to let your dog work out these issues with the other dogs, unless his reactions become profoundly hysterical or aggressive. After two or three trips to a dog park, most dogs not only learn to tolerate it but end up loving it.

A few words of caution, however. Before taking your dog into the park, check it out. Observe what type of dogs usually frequent it, and determine what the overall demeanor of the group is. Are the dogs unusually aggressive or unfair? Are they all much larger than your dog? Do they appear extremely unkempt or sickly in any way? Answering yes to these questions might be grounds to reconsider that particular dog park. If all the dogs are over sixty pounds but you have a Chihuahua, chances are your dog will spend most of his time there in mortal terror.

Try to pet some of the dogs present. Do any appear to have flea or tick infestations or skin disorders? These highly infectious problems could easily be passed on to your dog. Also, talk to the owners of the dogs, and try to ascertain if their pets have had all of the necessary inoculations, so that your pet does not become infected with a potentially fatal disease. For your dog's safety, make sure the other dogs are not overly aggressive, sick, infested, or in any way harmful to your canine friend.

Choose a day and time in which only six or seven other dogs are present. Weekday mornings are usually less crowded than weekends. At first, let your dog sniff the others from outside the fenced enclosure, just to see his reaction. If it appears all is well and your dog seems to want in, go ahead and lead him in, and then take him off the leash. There is no need to worry about your pooch running away; the fence will prevent that. Stay inside for a while to get a feel for the "pack" dynamic. If any dogs come up to you in a curious, playful manner, by all means say hello. Otherwise, try to be a passive observer. If your dog appears to be cautious and sticks by you for protection, take the lead and walk around the enclosure. This will ensure that your dog will interact with the others. Keep your leash at hand, but try to allow the dogs to work out their own hierarchy. If you do see uncalled-for aggression, call your dog over, clip on his leash, and leave. After all, as the leader of your dog's pack, you are ultimately responsible for his safety. Do not, however, brazenly confront a dog exhibiting aggressive intentions, as you and your dog could become injured. Just calmly remove yourself and your pet from the picture.

Herding Clubs

Any dog who has herding heritage in her genes can probably participate in this excellent form of exercise. Contact a local canine-training facility and ask about any local herding clubs; odds are they will be able to put you in contact with one, especially if you live in a rural or suburban area. Or call the American Kennel Club (AKC) at (919) 854-0199 for herding events and clubs in your region. If accepted, your dog will get to run with other dogs trained to herd a large flock of sheep. You will get to see your dog's natural herding instincts in operation, and your pet will have the time of her life.

Usually, only dogs with some herding heritage will be considered by the club. These include dogs with at least one parent from the following breeds:

- German shepherd
- Australian shepherd
- Border collie
- collie
- corgi
- Great Pyrenees
- Australian cattle dog
- puli
- komondor
- akbash
- Shetland sheepdog
- Belgian Tervuren
- Old English sheepdog
- Belgian Malinois

Other breeds can of course learn to herd, but club members often insist the dogs have at least some herding blood. Many dogs of other breed backgrounds can become too aggressive with the sheep, while others, particularly the smaller breeds, can become injured, often seriously.

This type of exercise takes quite a time commitment from you and your dog. You will have to participate at least once per week for months or more, until your dog learns the intricacies of the behavior. If you think your dog has what it takes, give one of these clubs a call. Not only will your dog burn incredible amounts of energy, but she will get in touch with an ancient, powerful instinct she was never able to express. (Note: Only dogs in excellent health will be accepted by a herding club. If your dog is obese, wait until her weight comes down before applying. Also, older dogs suffering from joint disorders shouldn't be asked to participate, as herding requires incredible agility and flexibility on the dog's part. Also, dogs showing any aggressive tendencies toward persons, sheep, or other dogs will not be allowed to participate.)

Cart or Sled Pulling

Some dog breeds have a history of pulling sleds or carts as a means of earning their keep. Rottweilers, mastiffs, and Saint Bernards have been used for centuries to pull carts, while arctic breeds such as Malamutes, huskies, Akitas, and Samoyeds have been used to pull sleds across snow and ice-covered territories.

If you have a large, powerful, big-boned dog, consider contacting a cart-pulling club, found through a local canine-training facility. Usually located in rural or suburban areas, the club will evaluate your dog to see if he meets the criteria. In addition to being large and strong, your dog will need to be friendly, cooperative, and willing to be strapped into a cart-pulling harness. No shy or aggressive dogs will be accepted. In addition, no dogs over seven or eight years of age will be allowed to participate, as cart pulling is extremely exhausting. Any dog participating cannot have joint, heart, or respiratory disorders.

If you live in a colder climate and own a large arctic breed, consider contacting a sled-pulling club. Bred to excel at this type of work, huskies, Samoyeds, Malamutes, and Akitas can all participate. If your arctic breed is healthy, strong, and filled with unquenchable energy, you might give it a try. Pulling as part of a team or singly, your dog will burn an unprecedented number of calories. Just make sure your dog has no aggressive tendencies toward other animals or persons.

Exercises for Cats

Kitty calisthenics? Not likely. Your cat *can* be lured into a wide variety of calorie-burning exercises, though, if you remain patient and committed. Although cats are certainly not as easily involved as dogs, the main obstacle to getting them going is the motivation factor. Whereas dogs are pack oriented and responsive to the desires of you, the pack leader, cats are for the most part independent beings, driven by relatively narcissistic motives. Though it's one of the main reasons we love them, this "I, me, mine" attitude does restrict what you can and cannot do with them.

In addition to their independent mind-set, a limitation to the feline learning curve is a restricted ability to adapt or modify their behavior, particularly in adult cats. In other words, cats are stubborn. Whereas dogs are malleable, cats are often intransigent. This makes it difficult to teach them new behaviors.

Difficult, yes, but not impossible. The friendly feline will respond to one tried-and-true motivator better than any other—food. Any cat with an average or better food drive will respond to behavior modification techniques quite well, if the reward used is tasty.

The problem with using food motivation to modify an overweight cat's behavior is obvious. This book, after all, is dedicated to pet weight loss; adapting a cat's behavior with too many treats can quickly defeat that purpose. How then can we teach a cat to participate in exercises without causing her to gain weight?

The answer is twofold. First, you need to ensure your cat will have a strong enough food drive to respond well to treat offerings. So, if you haven't already, you will need to heed my advice from the previous chapter and switch your cat from a free-feeding routine to a regular feeding schedule. By doing this, you will be able to better predict when your cat will be hungry. Your pet will begin to anticipate feeding time instead of simply wandering over to her bowl and picking at ever-present food. That anticipation, or heightened hunger drive, is what will allow you to train your cat with treats. The training sessions should take place right before feeding time, when the cat's food drive is at its strongest.

Second, because you will be heightening your cat's food drive through regular feeding times, the size of the treats will not need to be large. A small bit of cheese or a dollop of meat-flavored baby food is usually all it takes. Because cats have much less patience with repetitive training exercises than dogs, you will be working these new behaviors far fewer times than would be possible with a dog; therefore, fewer treats will be used.

Some exercises for cats will not necessitate much training, and as such will not call for the use of treats. A good number of exercises your cat might enjoy will be initiated by her own predatory instincts. Chasing erratic, fast-moving objects, for instance, will require little cajoling on your part. Other games will be fueled by the cat's desire to socialize with you, other family members, or other pets. Simple curiosity will also help you in your quest to get your kitty moving.

Climbing Stairs

As with dogs, you can get your cat to climb a flight or more of stairs each day if you just use the right motivation at the right time. Yes, you guessed it: food. Try placing his food dish upstairs at feeding time. This will require the cat to scurry up the stairs to eat. Likewise, you can place the dish downstairs in the basement, requiring the pet to descend to feed. If your cat doesn't seem to be able to find the new location, try moving the dish up only a few steps at first. Also, during the day, try randomly placing a small treat at the top (or the bottom) of the stairs. Over time this will teach the cat to frequently go up or down the stairs to investigate—and when he does, he will find a nice surprise. Eventually, the stair-climbing behavior will become a normal activity, helping you trim weight off your kitty.

Playing with Toys

Cats love to chase fast-moving, unpredictable objects, primarily due to the feline instinct to stalk and kill prey. Right from kittenhood, it becomes quite obvious to all cat owners just how strong a drive this is. You most likely have a few cat toys in the home right now, and perhaps you have some that are on the following list:

- teaser wands (a long thin rod with a wire- or spring-suspended feathery, furry tease-toy at the end)
- fake mouse toys
- tassel-type lures on a string
- macramé ball with catnip inside
- balled-up newspaper

- windup or battery-operated toys that scoot about the floor unpredictably
- toys suspended by a string from the ceiling or some other area of the home

Use any of these items on a regular basis to "rev up" your cat's behavior. Try to change the type of toy you use often, to keep the cat's interest level high. Try to surprise the cat with the toy, and do what you can to make it appear as if you have no control over the object. Bringing one out a half hour before feeding time will help improve your chances of getting the cat moving and interested, as the feline prey drive is strongest at this time.

The objective is to keep your cat moving and excited for at least ten minutes, to burn calories and get her muscles moving. Attempt these ten-minutes sessions at least four or five times per day. Enlist other members of the household to help you, especially if you are not home for a good part of the day. Of particular interest to most cats are those wind-up or battery-operated teaser toys that scamper all over the floor; they really get the cat going, without much input from you. Try one, and you'll be surprised at how active your cat can become.

Most cats will show a natural prey instinct to chase a thrown (or fleeing) object. Cats with particularly high stalk-ing drives should therefore do well with any type of toy-throwing game. Tease the cat for a minute with a ball or toy, until she becomes excited. When you have gotten the cat to swat or bite at the toy, give the object a short toss, right past the cat. Make sure the toy doesn't go too far the first time. If the cat goes after it and swats or mouths it, praise the cat with a small treat. Slowly increase the distance you throw the toy, continuing to reward any response with a treat. You may even get the cat to retrieve it! The objective is simply to get the cat involved and moving. Just remember not to overdo the treats, and to reduce the cat's regular feedings accordingly.

Your cat will respond more readily to this type of stimulation if you start when she is just a kitten. More than dogs, cats do not like change later in life. Don't despair, though; most adult cats will respond adequately to the right teaser toy. Just try a number of them until you find a few that light your cat's fire.

Random Placement of Small Treats

Compared to humans and dogs, who do not have much ability to leap high into the air, cats inhabit a three-dimensional world. Your cat probably spends time atop the refrigerator, bookcase, sofa, entertainment center, or any number of locations above ground level, which is a throwback to the wild cat's practice of sitting up high to observe his hunting ground. You can take advantage of this instinct and encourage vertical movement by your cat. Getting up high will require your cat to exert large amounts of energy jumping up and down. The large muscles in the rear half of your cat's body, if stimulated regularly, will burn lots of calories and raise the pet's metabolism.

Planting small, delectable treats in high-up spots your cat is known to frequent will encourage him to visit those areas more often, causing him to burn calories and build muscle. Again, don't use large treats, and try not to leave treats in the desired locations too regularly, as this will both keep the weight on your cat and lower his level of response. Remember: Infrequent, unpredictable reinforcement of a behavior will result in a better response than rewarding every time. Also, be careful not to encourage a cat to jump up to spots that have plants, picture frames, curtains, knickknacks, or anything fragile or dangerous. Lastly, do not encourage a seriously obese cat to jump up to (or down from) high places, as this can injure his musculoskeletal system. Instead, have the obese cat jump up to spots that are three to four feet high and no higher, until he loses most of the excess weight.

The Recall, or "Come"

Yes, cats can and do learn to come on command. Have you ever owned an outdoor cat who, though apparently out of sight, comes to the back door of your home as soon as you rap on the top of a cat food can with a fork? Even indoor cats become conditioned to come to the sound of an electric can opener in operation, thinking it's a can of delectable kitty food being opened.

Training your cat to come on command (or in the case of cats, on request) will, as with a dog, allow you to get your cat running whenever you so desire. She might be asleep upstairs when she hears you calling from the basement; she comes running, burning calories in the process. Remember: Anything you can do to get a cat moving will help the pet lose weight.

Teaching the recall or "come" command to a cat of course works much better when you start training at an early age. Kittens are more behaviorally malleable than adult cats, particularly with this type of "trick." Adult cats can, however, be taught to come, though not with the predictability of a dog. Any positive results should be considered a great victory on your part!

First, go to a variety store and purchase a child's "clicker" toy, the type that makes a snappy clicking sound when you press on it. Then, start teaching the recall to your cat by not feeding her dinner. Don't worry: Delaying one meal will in no way hurt her, and it might even be beneficial to the obese cat (see "Fasting" in chapter 3). Withholding one meal will ensure that the cat will be good and hungry, a prerequisite to teaching her to come to you. About one or two hours after her normal dinnertime, with the cat being held three or four feet away by a helper, get down on the floor with the clicker and a small dollop of cat food on a spoon. Simultaneously click the clicker repeatedly while offering the spoon of food to the cat and saying "come." Your helper should release your cat the moment you begin clicking. If she is at all hungry, she should come running. Repeat this three or four times, then quit for the evening. At this point you can feed the cat dinner; just be sure to reduce the quantity in relation to the amount of food used during the training.

Repeat the sessions two or three times each day. Lengthen the distance from the cat each time by a few feet, until, at the end of a few weeks, you are able to successfully get the cat to come to you from any part of the home or property. Make sure that each session occurs when the cat is hungry; reduce or delete meals accordingly, keeping in mind that the food fed to the pet during the session will make up for the lost meals. Also realize that, unlike with dogs, you will need to continue using food as an enticement, as praise alone won't cut it in the cat world. You should use infrequent rewards, however, after the cat has really mastered the behavior. Using food every other time should be sufficient to maintain the behavior.

Once you can get your cat to come to you on command

(or, more precisely, on "click"), you will be able to call her to you randomly, whenever you feel she needs some exercise. If you have properly taught your cat the trick, she should come running whenever you click. This will help get your cat moving and burning calories. It will also help stimulate her mind, decreasing the boredom factor; and as we've said, alleviating boredom is essential to weight loss.

Two Cats Are Better Than One

Though extremely independent in nature, cats do appreciate company, especially when accustomed to it from an early age. That's why you are so accepted by your cat. You are in effect a sibling or parent to him; and a cat will nearly always welcome the attentions and company of a "family" member, even while rejecting the attentions of others.

One of the best ways to keep your cat active while you are gone during the workday is to provide him with a feline companion. Having a playful partner around will pick up his activity level and stimulate his mind.

Unfortunately, many adult cats will simply not accept a new cat into the fold, due to the feline territorial instinct, which is on average stronger than that of a dog. Some of the worst cat aggression results from an owner innocently introducing a new cat or kitten into the home, a territory claimed and dominated by the original cat for years. So, how can you provide your cat with company without causing a fight?

Several possible solutions exist. The easiest is of course to get two kittens right from the start, preferably from the same litter. They will be quite accepting of each other and won't have developed that territorial bias yet. Quickly becoming inseparable, they will play and cavort like kittens well into adulthood. This heightened activity will help burn calories and keep their minds active.

If you have an adult cat, finding an acceptable companion can be difficult, but not impossible. If your cat has a history of tolerating other cats (or dogs), try introducing a four- or five-month-old kitten into the family. This age is important; the pet will be old enough to defend herself, yet immature enough to not be considered a big threat to the home cat.

At first, keep the new cat in a separate room, cloistered away from your adult cat. They will smell and hear each other, but won't be able to come face-to-face. This will help them become slowly accustomed to each other, without provocation. If you do not do this, the sudden invasion of the home cat's territory will almost assuredly cause aggression. After a few days of this, try to introduce the cats through a screen door or some other type of partition that allows them to see but not touch. Continue this for several days, and reward both cats with small treats whenever they can see each other in an attempt to teach them that the presence of the other cat is a good thing. Finally, allow them to be in the same room. At this stage it is really a hit-or-miss proposition. The home cat will most likely hiss a bit, and might not allow the new cat to approach for a while. Eventually, however, he should begrudgingly accept the new invader, provided the new animal does not commandeer the food dish or litter box.

To that end, make sure to purchase an additional food dish and a new litter box. Place them well away from the home cat's dish and box. Doing so will give each cat a safe place to eat and eliminate, two activities that can evoke the most heated territorial responses.

You can also try socializing your cat with a friendly dog.

Introducing them while very young, however, is highly recommended, as territorial disputes between these species can often end in death for the cat, or a damaged cornea for the dog.

Taking Your Cat for a Walk

No, this is not an April fool. Cats *can* learn to walk on a leash, if you start them out from kittenhood. Why, you ask, would you ever want to walk your cat on a leash? For several reasons. First, it's a good way to get your cat outside without jeopardizing her health or safety. Cats allowed to go outdoors on their own can end up contracting all manner of infectious diseases, including:

- feline immunodeficiency virus (FIV)
- feline infectious anemia
- feline leukemia (FeLV)
- feline infectious peritonitis (FIP)
- feline panleukopenia
- feline respiratory disease complex (FDRC)
- rabies
- conjunctivitis
- internal and external parasites

The occurrence of these often fatal diseases in cats has increased dramatically in the last decade, primarily because of the mistaken assumption that cats must be allowed to roam freely in order to stay psychologically fit, as well as the increased popularity of cats as pets. Additionally, the unwanted cat population has exploded, thanks to irresponsible owners who insist on letting their unneutered cats run free, allowing them to breed uncontrollably. (If you don't think this is a problem, just pay a visit to your local humane society, where thousands of unwanted kittens are put to sleep each month.) Decades ago, there were far fewer environmental dangers to cats living an indoor/outdoor life. In addition to the above-mentioned diseases, the increase in auto traffic is responsible for many cat deaths. Contrary to myth, cats do not lead charmed lives, and cannot magically avoid dangers any better than dogs. Clearly, letting your cat go outdoors without supervision is a good way to shorten her life.

The easiest way to keep your cat healthy is to keep her indoors. If raised inside, your pet will never crave the outdoors, and will happily claim your home as her territory. In addition to keeping her safe, you will be saving the lives of virtually hundreds of songbirds and other small creatures that your cat might otherwise prey upon.

Those owners who feel that it is not ethical to keep their cats indoors are simply allowing themselves to buy into a mistaken mystique about the feline. Would you ever allow your dog to roam freely in a busy environment? Why not? Your dog's wild brethren are just as capable of survival outdoors as any wild cat.

Allowing your cat supervised, occasional access to the great outdoors, however, can be a great thing for her mind and body. The outdoors can supply your cat with unlimited sensory stimulation and needed exercise, both vital to any weight loss plan. So, how can you provide your cat with *supervised* outdoor experiences?

The answer is to train her, from early kittenhood, to walk on a leash attached to a harness. Attempting to do so with an adult cat, will be a difficult and trying experience for you and your cat, so consider not beginning this with any cat over four or five months of age.

The first step is to purchase a cat harness from your local

pet shop. Fitting around the cat's midsection, this piece of equipment is vital to the exercise. No cat will tolerate having a leash attached to a collar; if any pressure is applied to her neck she will panic. Make sure the harness fits your kitten properly. The employees at the store can help you with this. Also, as the kitten grows, you may need to buy a larger harness; pay attention to this, as a tight harness can irritate or panic some cats.

When home with the kitten, let her see the harness, and reward her with a small treat whenever she comes close to it. Try smearing some cat food on the harness, encouraging the kitten to lick it. Do this for a day or two before moving on to the next step.

Next, place the harness on the kitten, loosely, for a minute or so, all the while rewarding the kitten with small treats. Slowly increase the time the harness is on the cat, until the pet is able to wear it with no worry or discomfort. Work on this slowly, for at least a week, before progressing further.

Then, attach a four-foot light leash to the harness, and let the cat walk around for a few minutes, dragging the leash in the process. Make sure the leash does not catch or tangle on anything, as this could panic the kitten. Slowly increase the time until the kitten has no concern about dragging the leash.

Then, pick up the end of the leash and slowly follow your kitten around the home, making sure not to put pressure on the leash. Just be a passive companion, and reward the kitten every few minutes with a small treat. Stay at this stage for at least two or three days.

Eventually, you should begin using slight pressure on the leash in an attempt to subtly direct the kitten. Under no circumstances, however, should you pull on the leash with any measurable force, as this could panic her. Unlike a dog, you are not trying to control the kitten's movements; you're simply preventing her from dashing away. The leash will act as a fail-safe device rather than a control feature.

Next, take the kitten out to a quiet backyard, and let her explore while on the leash. Consider at this point going to a longer leash, perhaps six to ten feet in length. Do so for a few minutes, reward her with a small treat, and then pick her up and go back inside. Continue to leave the harness on for at least half an hour each day, but leave the leash off. Slowly, over a period of a few weeks, increase the exploration time that you and your kitten spend in the backyard, until you are out for at least ten or fifteen minutes. Allow the kitten to explore; follow her around, letting her choose the route. The leash is there only to prevent the pet from dashing off; you should allow the kitten to control the experience. After ten or fifteen minutes, pick up the kitten and go back inside, always rewarding her with a small treat.

The experience need never go beyond this degree of exposure. If you choose to walk the kitten in a busier area, make sure to *very gradually* increase the level of exposure over weeks, not days. Do not take the kitten into a busy environment such as a city street. The object here is simply to get the cat outside in a controlled fashion. Remember that a cat will panic much faster than a dog, due to her highly individualistic nature.

This exercise is not for all cats. *Do not begin it with adult cats*, or with any kittens that seem to be shy or antisocial. If for any reason the cat becomes frightened or panicked, stop the activity. Go back to walking her indoors, or cease the exercise completely. The idea is to teach the cat very gradually, so that there is little chance of inducing fear. If your cat is outgoing and well adjusted, a daily walk around the backyard will be an enriching, calorie-burning experience.

Exercising the Older Pet

No cat or dog over eight or nine years of age should be pushed too hard physically. Older pets have, as do older humans, slower reaction times, and they suffer from stiffness and joint disorders. Working the older pet too hard can result in a higher incidence of injury. Also, your pet's aging cardiovascular and respiratory systems cannot support extended periods of exertion as well as those of a younger animal. Therefore, it is up to you to choose or modify the exercise your dog or cat gets according to his capabilities. Most of the aforementioned exercises can be used in moderation, though their frequency and duration will need to be reduced. Exercises such as hard running, long-distance jogging, extended swimming, or cart or sled pulling should be avoided, as these can be hard on the older pet's heart and joints. Consult with your veterinarian, and have him or her decide what would be allowable for your animal.

5. Behavioral Enrichment Programs

Relieve Boredom and Direct Your Pet's Instincts and Intellect

In the past, zoo animals, kept in barred cages with little else to do but eat and pace, often developed a host of physiological and behavioral problems, such as anorexia, obesity, neuroses, unpredictable aggression, antisocial behaviors, and lack of parenting skills. Removed from their natural habitats, wolves, lions, bears, elephants, and apes could not experience natural environmental stimuli, and often became listless and troubled.

Today, zoologists work hard to enrich the lives of captive zoo animals through innovative behavioral enrichment programs that attempt to relieve the boredom suffered by these wild creatures. Clever animal behaviorists design habitats and activities for these captive animals that come close to conditions in the wild. For instance, one zoo, in an attempt to stabilize a polar bear's eating habits and relieve his boredom, simply stocked his pool with trout. The bear quickly became enthralled with this new edible stimulus, deftly learning to catch and eat the fish. This simple addition to the bear's environment gave him something to do that mirrored what might occur in the wild. It engaged his mind and gave him purpose, something all animals need to feel happy and confident.

Domestic cats and dogs need to feel they too have a purpose. Unfortunately, most of them live in environments that closely resemble those of captive zoo animals from the forties and fifties. Their territories are minute compared to what they would be in the wild, and the behavioral stimuli offered to them are nearly nonexistent. Their natural instincts to hunt, stalk, play, or investigate are rarely engaged. Most family pets spend their time sleeping, wandering around an empty home waiting for the owners to come home, or pacing back and forth inside a fenced-in enclosure in the backyard, much like a stir-crazy zoo leopard or coyote. Starved of sensory input and intellectual stimulation, these pets often fixate on the only activity readily available to them: eating. Owners often do not relieve their pet's boredom even when they are home, as they themselves fall into predictable behavior patterns that often exclude any thought of the pet's mental well-being.

In an attempt to occupy their pet's time, many owners provide food on a continuous basis. As discussed earlier, this free-feeding practice often leads to compulsive overeating, resulting in obesity. Pets in this type of situation can come to see eating as their sole purpose in life. Consequently, they become obsessed with food and pay attention to little else.

If zoologists can invent behavioral enrichment programs that help minimize the boredom and neuroses of captive zoo animals, so too can we for domestic cats and dogs. By inventing and introducing simple activities that challenge and stimulate the domestic pet's mind and body, owners can give their dogs and cats a feeling of purpose, and temporarily take their minds *off food*, perhaps for the first time in their lives. These activities occupy the pet's time, teach focus and problem-solving skills, create a sense of purpose, utilize the pet's natural intelligence and curiosity, and serve as an outlet for pent-up energy and stress. A calmer, happier, more directed pet will not become bored, grouchy, and listless, conditions that lead to overeating and other disadvantageous behaviors.

This section will offer numerous easy-to-provide behavioral stimuli that will help relieve your pet's boredom, stimulate her mind, and redirect her away from eating. Though many of the behavioral enrichment activities can and will burn calories and help raise the pet's metabolism, they differ somewhat from exercise in that their primary purpose is to expand the animal's sensory and intellectual parameters, creating a calmer, happier, better-adjusted dog or cat, with a reduced need to fixate on food. Some of the activities discussed will apply to dogs, others to cats, and some to both. You can try out any of the activities, or attempt to create your own.

Behavioral Enrichment Activities for Dogs

Socialize Your Dog

One of the most common mistakes we unknowingly make with our dogs is to isolate them from other dogs and humans. Canines are among the most sociable creatures on the planet; in the wild, their very existence depends on a well-defined pack relationship, with many members working in concert, the goal being the acquisition of large, fast-moving prey animals. Unfortunately, we often keep our dogs at home, alone, for more than ten hours each day, a highly unnatural condition for a canine. Then, after we come home from a hard day's work, we often interact only minimally with our pooches.

Dog owners should attempt to socialize their pets as much and as regularly as possible, from puppyhood through adulthood. Right from the start, try to involve your dog with neighbors, relatives, family members, and anyone who might come into your dog's life on a regular basis, such as the mail carrier. The bigger the pool of individuals, the better. Have these individuals greet your dog with a small treat, then interact in a fun, nonthreatening way, perhaps playing fetch, or simply taking the dog for a quick walk. Try taking your dog for regular walks in active areas, so that he can see people and goings-on. If your dog is friendly and confident, allow him to greet people along the way. Carry some small, low-calorie treats with you, and allow the people you meet to give your dog a treat in exchange for a happy greeting, or perhaps a "sit." Praise your dog with a pat each time he greets someone happily. *Do not attempt this, however, if your dog has any history of aggression toward people, as it could result in a biting incident.* If you have a fearful, shy dog, simply take him for walks in areas where people and activity can be seen from a distance. Doing so on a regular basis will allow your pooch to slowly become desensitized to crowds.

Socialize your dog with other dogs as often as possible, as long as he does not show any dog-aggressive tendencies. As mentioned in chapter 4, the local dog park is a great place to socialize your pet with other dogs. Walking him on a regular basis with a neighbor and his or her dog is also a good tradition to start. Try to initiate a "block dog walk" at least once a week. Simply have three or four dog-owning neighbors and their dogs accompany you and your pooch on a fifteen-minute stroll around the block. The companionship and excitement of the event will brighten up your dog's entire day. Again, do not attempt this if your dog (or any other in the group) shows any kind of aggression.

Try either to get home for ten minutes during the day or have a friendly neighbor come over to your home for a few minutes to greet and play with your dog. Even a five-minute midday visit will be an unexpected break in your dog's otherwise dull day.

Provide Your Dog with Safe Chew Toys

One great way to help occupy your dog's day while you are gone is to provide her with a few safe chew toys. Dogs love to chew, and they will usually find something to gnaw on, whether provided by you or not. Chewing will help your pooch pass the time and give her a pleasurable activity. Also, providing a proper chew toy will help prevent any destructive activity from occurring. Bored dogs (especially young ones) have a tendency to find a shoe, remote control, purse, or favorite piece of clothing and chew it to smithereens, much to your dismay. It will usually be an article that you either handle or wear often, as it will contain much of your scent, something your dog knows and loves. "Dog-proof" the home by removing any and all of your personal objects from dog level, and replacing them with two or three safe dog chew toys. These include:

- *Hard rubber or nylon bones, rings, or other safe toys purchased at the pet store.* To make these more enticing, boil them in chicken stock for ten minutes. The dog will enjoy the flavor and will be more likely to accept these nonnatural chews. Repeat the boiling process once per week to keep up the dog's interest.

- *Smoked pigs' hooves or ears.* Your dog will love these natural chews and will eagerly use them with no prompting from you. The hooves will last longer than the ears, and they are usually a bit cheaper. Purchase either at your local pet shop. They don't smell all that wonderful to us, but dogs love them. Do not, however, use these or any other natural chew with a dog that shows any type of food-aggressive or overly possessive tendencies, as they can amplify the problem. If you have a hard time taking something away from your dog, avoid all natural chew products and contact an experienced canine behaviorist.

- *Rope toys.* Many dogs like to chew on thick braided rope toys, available at the local pet shop. If yours does, leave one on the floor. The only drawback to these is that the texture of the rope is very similar to certain rugs or types of clothing. If your dog has a habit of chewing on fabrics or carpets, avoid rope toys.

For health reasons, a number of chews available in stores should not, in my opinion, be provided to your dog. *Rawhide chews,* made from cured beef skin, should be avoided because they have a tendency to substantially expand in size once in the dog's stomach. A two-by-one-inch piece, swallowed by your pooch, can quadruple in size once in the stomach, potentially causing a life-threatening blockage. (To prove this, try leaving a rawhide bone in a bucket of hot water for eight or ten hours. The results may shock you.) *Avoid real bones,* particularly cooked poultry bones, as these can splinter and cause grave problems. Even large knucklebones that do not splinter should not be used regularly, as over time they can wear down the dog's teeth prematurely. I can always tell when a client's dog has been given a regular supply of bones just by looking at her teeth. A five- or six-year-old pet who regularly chews on bones will almost always have the dentition of a dog twice her age; the teeth are worn down far ahead of their time. If you must give knucklebones, do so only infrequently. Also, avoid giving bones to any dog who is food aggressive or overly possessive with toys or chews. A bone will cause this type of dog to greedily covet it, and she might bite anyone or anything trying to take the valuable possession away. Again, if your dog has a problem with possessiveness or food aggression, see a trained canine behaviorist.

Trick Training

Teaching your dog as many tricks as possible will expand his mind and teach him to *think*. Most untrained dogs do not think as much as *react* to stimuli; and this nonthinking mind-set can create a bored and destructive pet. Take a tricks class at the local humane society, or buy a few books on the subject. You and your dog will learn much about each other, and your dog will have another outlet besides eating. Some easy, basic tricks you can teach your dog include:

Sit

To teach your dog this trick, hold a delectable treat in your closed hand and let the dog sniff it. Then, raise your hand up slowly, right above and slightly behind your dog's head, while saying "sit." In attempting to follow the treat with her nose, your dog should automatically sit. Make sure not to move the treat forward, as this will cause the dog to walk toward the treat, or jump up. When your dog sits to get better access to the treat, let her have it while saying "good sit." Eventually your rising hand will become the hand sign for the trick.

SPIN

To get your dog to spin around in a circle, hold a treat in front of his nose. Then, while saying "spin," slowly move the treat in a wide circle around the dog, in an attempt to get him to follow it around himself. Your goal is to have the dog's nose planted on your treat-holding hand, all the way around. Start this out slowly, and always give the dog the treat if he even partially responds. The idea is to eventually lure him around in a full circle. Gradually, as the dog gets the idea, you should stop luring him all the way around the circle, and instead just initiate the movement, then step away slightly and see if he will complete the circle on his own. The objective is to train the dog to perform the trick on his own, as soon as you say "spin." As you begin to distance yourself from the dog, try to incorporate a slight spinning motion with the hand holding the treat. This will become the hand sign for the trick.

Move the Food Dish

Wolves do not find prey in the same spot each time. They have to seek it out, using all the sensory gifts given to them. Try the same thing with your dog. Every few days, instead of feeding her in the same spot (usually the kitchen), move the dish to a completely different place, perhaps the bathroom or the upstairs hallway. At first your dog will be confused and perhaps slightly miffed, but she will eventually catch on and find the food using her nose. Playing this little game will really get your dog thinking and using her senses.

Temporary Change of Territory

Your dog's territory is infinitely smaller than a wolf's in the wild. Often limited to the home and a small backyard, your canine friend never gets to exercise his senses to the fullest and is denied a host of experiences that come naturally in a vast territory. As a result, your dog can become bored, resulting in more food eaten.

In an attempt to stimulate your dog's senses and reduce his reliance on eating as his only meaningful activity, consider temporarily changing his territory. Do so by simply allowing the dog to spend a day or two at a friend or relative's home, one with which your pet is familiar. The new scents and surroundings will recharge the dog's mind and give him lots to think about besides kibble. If possible, spend this time with your dog. Doing so will allow you to see him relate and adapt to the new environment, always a fun and educational experience. Your presence will also comfort the dog if at first he seems uncomfortable or worried about the new territory. If your dog is gregarious and confident, feel free to leave him with the new person for a day or two. If he lacks confidence and seems to suffer from separation anxiety, consider staying with him in the new place.

A variant of this territorial change is to take the dog with you on short or long road trips. If you are planning a camping trip, for instance, consider going to an area that allows dogs. The change of scenery and the outdoor experience can do wonders for your dog's physical and mental well-being. Even a ten-minute trip to the store can be a welcome break in the monotony for many dogs. So, next time you have to scoot off to the store for some supplies, think about taking your four-legged buddy along for the ride. Just make sure that you do not leave your pooch unattended for too long inside a car, especially on a warm day. Also, leave a window open at least an inch or two, even on a cool day, so the dog can get some fresh air.

Leave on a Radio or Television

Often something as simple as leaving a radio or television on while you are gone during the day can serve as a great comfort to a dog spending the entire day alone. The sound of conversation or music, if kept at a tolerable volume, will create a sense of company for the dog, and cater to her auditory sense. Try leaving a radio on in a room with the door closed; this will create the illusion that someone just might be home sleeping or resting behind the closed door. This technique is almost a must for a puppy or young dog forced to be alone for extended periods. Also, consider purchasing a "doggy video" for your pet. Pet shops sell these animal videos, which contain images of dogs, cats, and other animals cavorting around, as close to life size as possible. Don't laugh: Many dogs actually love watching.

Objects with Food Inside

Some zoos have provided their resident bears with old spare tires that have peanut butter smeared all over the inside surface. The bears spend hours trying to get at the tasty treat inside the tire, thereby keeping themselves involved and happy. You can do the same with your dog. Start with a tennis ball: Cut a small slit into it and stick a small piece of food inside, or use the peanut butter trick. Leave the ball out for your dog and watch how he reacts. Odds are he will spend lots of time trying to get to the prize inside. This works well with most dogs, but may not be a great idea for pets who have a tendency to rip up and eat tennis balls or other toys, as swallowing pieces of it could cause serious blockages in the digestive tract. If your dog has this problem, consider using a more indestructible object, such as a long, narrow steel or hard plastic cup, or a durable rubber toy purchased at your local pet shop, one with a hollow center that can house a treat or a dab of peanut butter. For strong dogs kept in the yard or in a fenced enclosure, try the bear tactic. Get an old spare tire, coat the inside of it with peanut butter, and let your pooch go at it. Big powerful dogs such as rottweilers, pit bulls, mastiffs, or Great Danes will find this an irresistible way to spend time.

Food Frozen in Ice

Try giving your dog frozen cubes or blocks of ice that have food imbedded in them. Use something really desirable, such as a ball of canned food or cheese. Also, instead of using water as the ice base, try chicken broth. Your dog will lick away at the tasty frozen ice until she gets to the prize inside. This will keep her busy and happy for quite some time.

Raw Egg, Still in the Shell

This is a fun one, especially for a dog who has never encountered an egg before. Instead of feeding him a normal meal, simply leave one whole egg, still in the shell, in his food dish. Then, watch your pooch work out the problem. Because the shell is porous, the egg will have a scent, so he will certainly know that this strange object is in fact food. Getting to the prize inside may take him a while, but that process is exactly what you want to occur; let your pet figure it out. When he finally cracks the egg open, watch his reaction. You will almost be able to hear him cheer!

Mirrors

If your dog has to spend lots of time alone, consider buying several large unbreakable mirrors and distributing them around the home at dog level. Most dogs do not realize their reflections are themselves; looking at their image can be quite entertaining and engaging. Just make sure your dog does not react aggressively to the new "stranger", as this could cause her to become destructive.

Dog Crates

Within every wolf pack's territory is at least one den, a relatively snug enclosure either dug into a hillside or adapted from a cave. Though their territory is vast, wolves rely on this den for shelter, warmth, protection, and comfort. Many dog owners, not aware of the denning instinct of their pets, do not provide them with small secure little "havens" to go to for privacy or for resting. If your dog stays home all day, provide him with a plastic crate, to use as a private sanctuary. Place a soft blanket inside, and set it up in a quiet section of the home. This will give your pooch a place to go when he wants to rest or escape times of boisterous activity, such as when groups of small children visit the home. Having a place to go to will comfort the dog and create a small area or territory he can call his own. This will boost morale and help him adjust to life within the territory of another (namely you). And a happier dog is less likely to obsess on food.

Additional Behavioral Enrichment Activities for Your Dog

The list of inspiring, mind-expanding activities in which your dog can participate is long, and limited only by your imagination. As discussed in chapter 4, you can enroll your dog in an *agility class*, letting her play and compete against other dogs while learning how to run an obstacle course. Or, you can enroll your pooch in a *tracking class*, in which dogs learn to find people or objects solely by scent, on a fairly large course. *Herding classes*, for the appropriate breed, can also be very fulfilling and enjoyable for many dogs. Even a traditional *obedience class*, attended once per week, can really get your dog's creative and social juices going, while also teaching her good manners.

Use your imagination and your firsthand familiarity with your dog in trying to invent behavioral enrichment activities for her. Does your pooch have a keen nose? Take advantage of that when designing an activity. For example, leave a trail of treats down on the floor, leading to a special prize. The same goes for a dog with a high prey drive, or herding instinct. Decide what your dog is naturally good at, and then design a behavioral enrichment activity to suit her. By keeping your dog thinking and involved, you will help relieve her boredom and get her mind off dinnertime. You will also get to see the innate intelligence of your pooch shine through, a quality all but ignored in most of today's canine pets.

Behavioral Enrichment Activities for Cats

Your feline friend needs to be involved and mentally stimulated as much as any dog. Unfortunately, most pet cats are supplied with even less behavioral or environmental stimuli than the average dog, primarily because owners falsely assume that cats are completely able to amuse themselves, with no help from us lowly humans. Because of the feline penchant for independence, we simply leave cats to their own devices, convinced that they can generate their own fun. Not true! Indoor cats especially suffer from a tremendous lack of environmental stimuli, resulting in an increased level of boredom and a heightened fixation on food, as eating becomes one of the few activities left to the poor cat.

Many of the behavioral enrichment activities used to spice up a dog's life can also work for a cat. Some, however, are not appropriate, due to the cat's less sociable nature and restricted willingness to learn new behaviors. The following are some behavioral enrichment activities that you can try with your cat.

Socialize Your Cat

Try to involve other persons in your cat's life from as early a time as possible, to allow him a wider spectrum of experience. If possible, have a neighbor, friend, or relative come over during the day, while you are at work, to interact with the cat. Having them offer a small treat to the pet will help ingratiate themselves with your pet.

If at all possible, involve other animals in your cat's life. Though most cats will accept another pet only if they have grown up together, some will tolerate other cats if the visitor poses no threat (in your cat's mind) to his territory. The best solution is to get two kittens instead of one, and let them bond right from the start. The partnership they develop will help stimulate them mentally for years to come.

Tricks

Though not as adept at learning as dogs, your cat can learn to perform behaviors such as "come" or "beg." Simply sound a clicker, bell, whistle, or buzzer each time you feed the cat. After a few weeks, sound the device at a time other than feeding time, and watch your cat come running. Or, at random times, tempt your cat into a begging position (sitting back on her haunches with front paws high up) by offering her a small delectable treat. Lure her into the begging position by keeping the treat a few inches from her nose, until she reaches the proper posture. Then give her the treat. The purpose of this activity is to get the cat thinking about cause and effect, thereby stimulating her mind.

Toys

Cats are superior predators. Unfortunately, most owners do not provide their cats with opportunities to express this natural instinct. One great way to enrich your cat's world is to provide him with toys and objects that cater to this predatory calling.

First, try leaving a few *catnip-filled crocheted balls* in various places around the home. These will excite your cat and give him something to look forward to each day. Make sure to move them around the home, so as not to let the process become predictable.

If you really want to excite your cat, purchase a small

train set. Set it up in a corner of your home, and turn it on a few times each day. Your cat will switch into predatory mode and pounce on the fleeing choo-choo. Make sure to turn it on only a few times each day, for only a few minutes at a time, so that the cat does not become desensitized to the activity.

As discussed in chapter 4, supply your cat with some *teaser toys,* such as small mice or feather lures on the end of a string or wand. At random times, pull one out and tease your cat with it. Get the pet to chase and eventually catch it, and then put it away. Keeping your cat's predatory instincts honed in this way will help get his mind off food.

Or think about investing in a few *windup or battery-operated toys,* available at any good pet shop. Many of these can be extremely exciting and motivating to even the most staid cat; the toys move around the floor in an erratic fashion, much the way a fleeing mouse might. Purchase a few, and, at random times during the day, turn them on and watch your cat turn into a real tiger!

Aquariums

Placing a small aquarium in your home will really get your cat's predatory juices going. A ten- or twenty-gallon tank with five or six small fish is all you'll need; your cat will watch them with hunger and fascination. Just make sure the top of the tank is *securely* closed off from probing paws. The pet shop employee you buy the tank from will help you decide on a tank cover that will help prevent the untimely demise of the captive fish. Your cat will completely forget about her food dish and watch the fish the way we watch the television.

Move the Cat's Food

As with a dog, you can stimulate your cat's mind and senses by randomly moving his food dish around the home once or twice each week. Initially he will be confused; eventually, though, he will catch on. At first, move the dish only a few feet. Then move it to another room, and eventually across the home. Do not do it on a daily basis, however; just try it once or twice per week, as cats can become more upset than dogs by a consistently unpredictable environment.

Change Territories

Allowing your cat to visit a friend or relative's house every once in a while will stimulate her inquisitive nature and enrich her mind. Bring your kitty over to the "guest" home and let her explore for an hour or so, and then bring her home. Try not to bring your cat into the home of another pet, however, unless they have a history of being friendly to each other; cats do not react well to an invasion of their territories. Also, don't leave the cat in her new surroundings for more than an hour without bringing along a litter box. It's a good idea to try this for short periods at first, observing the pet's reactions. Extremely shy or antisocial cats probably won't deal well with this technique, though outgoing felines should have no problem.

Radio or Television

As with dogs, leaving a radio or television on during the day can keep a solitary cat company. Keep the volume low, and try to find a station with lots of talk and little music. The human banter will give the cat the sense of you or someone else being present. You can increase the effect by using a radio or television in a closed room, which will support the illusion that you are inside, talking with someone. Since the cat cannot get into the room, he cannot prove you are not there. This piques his interest and keeps him thinking.

As with dogs, you can purchase "kitty videos" that can excite and stimulate your cat. Scenes of other cats or animals are shown, with the animals filmed appearing as close to life size as possible. Many cats love watching these videos.

Food Inside an Object

Placing a small treat inside of a ball (preferably one the cat cannot rip apart and eat) can occupy a solitary cat's time quite well. Also, as with dogs, leaving down a few ice cubes with food imbedded inside can really keep a cat busy. Again, using chicken broth to make the ice instead of water will ensure your cat's attention.

Mirrors

Leaving a few unbreakable mirrors around the home at cat level can get your cat excited and involved. Move them around the home, and pick them up every now and then to keep your cat on her toes.

Kitty Condos

Many pet shops sell large, carpeted "kitty condos" that cats just love to explore or rest in. Consisting of a fairly large carpeted enclosure with various attached perches and platforms, most cats welcome the interesting new distraction such structures bring. Entice your cat into or onto one by randomly leaving small treats inside the enclosure or on one or more of the platforms. Like a crate for a dog, a kitty condo can become a place of security and comfort for your pet.

Scratching Posts

Every cat should have at least two scratching posts. Cats have an instinctive need to scratch, for a number of reasons. Scratching helps the cat shed worn claw coverings, a natural process that needs to occur on a regular basis. Also, all cats, from lions right down to tabbies, instinctively want to visually mark out their territories by placing scratch marks on objects close to their territorial boundaries. It's sort of a way to say "no trespassing!" to other cats in the area.

Your cat needs to satisfy his instinctive need to scratch; without this, he will become stressed and destructive. If you don't provide your cat with a preferred place to scratch, he will choose a location on his own—usually an expensive piece of furniture. To prevent your sofa or recliner from becoming the object of your cat's attentions, provide him with a couple of tall scratching posts that are at least three feet high, four to six inches wide, and covered with carpeting or some other textured material. A six-inch-wide log with the bark left on works well, as does a four-by-four-foot length of lumber wrapped with thick, coarse hemp rope. In addition to satisfying the cat's need to shed claw coverings and mark territory, scratching will help relieve boredom.

Place one scratching post near where the cat sleeps, as cats tend to like to stretch and scratch as soon as they wake up. Place the other in an area near your favorite pieces of furniture; this way, your cat will have a desirable alternative to ripping up your couch or chair. Encourage the cat to use these scratching posts from an early age by actually getting down on the floor and scratching at them yourself.

Boxes

Cats love exploring cardboard boxes, especially those with wadded-up newspaper inside. A simple environmental enrichment tool, most cats will spend lots of time crawling in and out of one. Simply get a good-sized box from the supermarket, place some wadded-up newspaper inside it, and put the box in the middle of a room. To make it all the more exciting, place a few treats inside as well. After the cat has begun to show an interest, move the box to another part of the home. This will keep the activity exciting. To really get the cat motivated, let her play in the box for ten or fifteen minutes, put the box away for a few days, and then give it to her again, this time with a battery-operated or windup mouse inside the box!

Open the Curtains on a Window

Simply opening the curtains or shades on a window can help stimulate an indoor cat. Being able to watch the goings-on of the neighborhood will enrich his mind and help relieve boredom. Seeing a squirrel or sparrow cavorting right outside the window will surely take his mind off that dish of kibble!

Food Trail

Every so often, leave a trail of small bits of food winding through the home, leading to some prize, such as a bit of tuna or a piece of cheese. Let the trail wind upstairs and around corners. The "hunt" will excite and stimulate your cat. Just be sure not to use large treats, or to practice this every day, as it could add too many calories and result in a fat cat. Be sure to subtract the calories contained in these treats from the cat's daily allotment.

Quail Eggs

Cats in the wild love stumbling across a nest of eggs. Nutritious and tasty, they provide wild cats with high amounts of protein and other needed nutrients.

Your domestic cat can also benefit from these small prizes. Expecting your cat to be able to break into a chicken egg might be asking a lot, though, as they tend to be a bit too large for the cat's jaws and teeth. As an answer, go to your butcher or to an Asian market, where smaller quail or pigeon eggs should be available. Instead of feeding your cat her regular meal one day, leave a few of these tiny eggs in the dish. The first time you do so, poke a hole in one of the eggs, to let the cat know what's in them. Some cats might not catch on, but most will be fascinated by the challenge and the reward. This activity will enrich your cat's feeding experience, and get your buddy thinking about problems and solutions, just as cats in the wild are forced to do. Bon appétit, kitty!

Distribute Various Scents Throughout the Home

Although it is not as keen as a dog's, your cat's sense of smell is much stronger than your own. Accordingly, any environmental enrichment program would be incomplete without some type of olfactory stimulus. To that end, try stimulating your cat's sense of smell by depositing various scents throughout the home. Rub a piece of cheese on the corner of a table leg; put a drop of fish oil on a small piece of paper towel and leave it on top of a bookcase. Just a little will do. This will stimulate your cat's senses and mind, and help her be more like her wild cousins.

Letting Your Cat Outdoors?

I want to say just a word about letting your cat outdoors. My feeling on the matter is that it is a good way to get your cat killed, or infected with a potentially fatal disease. A domestic cat is not a magician or a wizard; he cannot defy nature, but only live within it. Outdoor cats live shorter lives, get injured far more often, get "kidnapped" by other well-meaning persons, become infested with internal and external parasites, and breed unnecessarily. You wouldn't allow your dog or your child out by herself, so why let your cat out?

Try as I might to get this point across, some owners and cat enthusiasts will insist that for a cat to be mentally healthy, he needs to go out and explore. If that is your belief, then so be it. Keep in mind, however, that a cat let outdoors in an urban environment will almost surely not live out a normal life span. And, contrary to popular belief, a cat kept indoors all his life, if provided with the proper level of environmental enrichment, will be absolutely fine. Understand that long ago, when we decided to domesticate dogs and cats, we purposely changed their lives forever. They now have little choice but to depend on us for survival. Because that is so, we should ensure our cats' good health and survival by keeping them indoors, or taking them outside only under supervised conditions, such as on a harness, in a car, or in a secure yard with an unclimbable fence, high enough to prevent them from escaping.

Choosing the Right Enrichment Program

Whether you own a dog, a cat, or both, you know your pet better than anyone else. Use that intimate knowledge to choose the proper environmental enrichment activities for her. For instance, if you know your pet hates being around other animals, avoid activities that require this of her, and choose instead some of the many activities mentioned that encourage independent action. If your pet excels in an area such as athletic participation, opt for activities that encourage this ability, such as tracking, agility, or any other involving great expenditures of energy. Remember also to consider the pet's age and physical restrictions; don't force an old or diminutive pet to participate in something she can't do without hurting herself.

Besides considering your dog or cat's physiological and psychological limitations, consider her likes and dislikes. Pets are like humans in that they often have definite preferences based on their personalities. Don't force your shy Persian to socialize with the loud neighbors next door. Do encourage your gregarious, sweet-tempered Labrador retriever to fetch a ball or play with the neighbor's collie. Above all, be aware of your pet's personality, and work from there. Be inventive and positive, and always strive to make your dog or cat's life an interesting and fulfilling one, instead of a boring series of meals connected by mindless inactivity. In doing so, you will be helping to decrease her reliance on food, and her propensity to gain weight.

6. Train Your Pet

How Establishing Leadership and Behavioral Boundaries Helps Stabilize Your Pet's Food Drive and Creates a Confident, Secure Mind-Set

All pets need some level of training to integrate properly into their human families. A pet must quickly learn which behaviors are acceptable and which are not. Though cats and dogs have differing capabilities and expectations with regard to sociability and hierarchical structure, both species can and should be taught to understand what is allowable and what is inappropriate. If not taught this by the owner, the dog or cat can easily become a leaderless, out-of-control bully, and the owner a disgruntled, subservient, lesser member of the "pack," there only to provide the pet with food, shelter, and amusement.

Poorly trained dogs or cats who have taken control of the household often become obese, as they normally get what they want, including excess food or treats. An owner with poor control over his or her pet will often attempt to bribe the animal with food to cajole him into behaving. At other times, hapless owners will simply give in to an untrained, dominant pet's demands for scraps, treats, or increased portions at dinnertime.

This chapter will show you how to establish fundamental leadership and control over your pet. Instead of bribing an obese, dominant pet with food, you will learn fundamental ways to gain leadership and loyalty as tools to control and guide your canine or feline companion.

Leadership: What It Is, and Why It Is Essential to Your Pet's Well-Being

All mammals, be they tigers, wolves, bears, otters, or humans, recognize some level of leadership within their species and in their everyday lives. Though leadership roles are more highly developed within the canine world, both cats and dogs must quickly identify and participate willingly in some type of hierarchical social order. They have to, for the survival of the species. For example, every wolf pack has a clearly defined hierarchy of leadership. Developing a chain of command, from the all-important alpha male right down to fringe members of the pack, allows the group to function efficiently and quickly, with little contention. A well-run wolf pack is much more likely to coordinate a successful hunt than one with no clearly defined leadership structure. Dissension among the wolves would mean fewer prey animals killed, and a higher likelihood of starvation for the members. This militaristic approach ensures the wolves will be able to act in concert with each other when going for the kill. In addition, it ensures that the strongest members of the pack will breed, guaranteeing that the genes most essential to survival are passed on to future offspring. Without the dominant members of the pack controlling the mating process, physically or mentally inferior wolves would be produced, ultimately leading to increasingly less capable pack members.

Though cats in the wild are by nature much more independent than dogs, leadership controls exist for them as well. Even with totally independent species such as the snow leopard or the puma, an instinctive understanding of dominance and leadership is maintained.

During the first year of life, most cats interact with their siblings and mother on an almost continuous basis. The youngsters play with each other for hours at a time, not only for the joy of play, but also to learn hunting, stalking, and survival skills, and to develop needed social skills used later in life. During adulthood, others of their kind will invariably approach, either to quarrel over territory or to mate. Without learning some rudimentary social skills early in life, successful interactions would not be possible.

During the early social stages of a wild cat's life, she learns just what dominance and submission mean. A few of the young cats in the litter are always bigger and stronger than the others; these siblings play rougher, and often feed first, further accelerating their growth. The smaller, weaker cats have no choice but to submit to their more assertive kindred. Once grown, wild cats go out on their own and live a relatively solitary life, although they still defer to the social hierarchy. The cats who were dominant in their litter will invariably see themselves as dominant over any other cat they meet later in life.

Your dog or cat identifies himself as one of the members of the group living in your home. A dog will see himself as one of the "pack," while a cat usually identifies herself either as your sibling or your offspring. Where your pet positions himself in the hierarchy will to a large degree determine his behavior toward you, as well as his demands and expectations. For instance, a dog who sees himself as dominant over his owner may think it perfectly okay to growl or even bite, as these are normal behaviors of dominant dogs in a pack. The leader has a duty to keep order and define the rules. If you don't do it, your dog will.

The same holds true for cats, though in a slightly different way. Domestic cats normally see their owners as either siblings or parents. If you come across as a dominant yet fair provider of food, shelter, and affection, chances are your cat will relate to you as a child relates to a parent. However, if you appear as an equal or a submissive, your cat may consider you a lesser sibling, loved but dominated. In this case, the cat may decide that she calls the shots, and that she should be entitled to first dibs on anything in the home, including food, attention, or a choice resting area.

If your dog or cat decides you are anything but the dominant animal in the home, you will begin to experience behavioral problems with him. A dominant dog or cat will try to monopolize your attentions, or scold you when you pet him at a time when he wants to be alone. The pet will show affection or aggression on a whim, and will claim any or all areas in the home, including beds, chairs, tables, or any other desirable spots. He may even decide to eliminate wherever he wants, even if that place is under your bed, or on the living-room carpet. What's most important to the theme of this book is that a dominant, untrained cat or dog will lay claim to any food available in the home, whether it be pet food or people food.

The only control a hapless submissive owner thinks he or she has over such a domineering pet is food bribery. So the untrained, pushy, dominant cat or dog ends up learning that misbehavior on her part will ultimately result in a food reward. It is no accident, then, that so many overweight cats and dogs are also behavioral nightmares. They have their owners trained well, and they know that the most common response to their obnoxious behavior will be treats, table scraps, and second helpings of pet food.

To prevent your pet from becoming a pushy little beggar and an overall behavioral nightmare, you need to set ground rules right from the start. Asserting your dominance through the establishment and enforcement of basic behaviors and rules will teach your dog or cat who is in charge, and will help prevent dominant pushy behavior, including incessant begging. A well-behaved, respectful pet won't need to be continually lured out of disobedience with cookies or other treats. He will respect your leadership, and your house rules. Sounds easy, right?

Basic Leadership and Training for Your Dog

Dogs are smart, adaptive creatures who, unlike cats, *want* to belong to a cohesive pack. That said, if given the chance, every dog would choose to be the leader of her group. That means your dog will quickly become dominant over you if allowed.

To be a just, fair, responsible dog owner, you must be the leader of your pack. In doing so, you will make your dog's life easier and less stressful. A dog with a competent leader to rely on will be less apt to suffer from stress and will be far less likely to show aggression. In addition, a dog who can easily identify her leader will be far less likely to have other behavioral problems, ranging from destructive behavior or improper house-training to obsessive-compulsive disorders (such as incessant barking or licking sores) or overeating. Dogs with competent and caring leaders are calmer, more relaxed, and less obnoxious.

The following are some very basic rules and techniques you can apply to your dog, to help her clearly understand that you are the leader. Starting these as early as possible will ensure that the relationship between you and your pet remains one with you squarely in the position of "benevolent dictator," and not trusted servant. Keep in mind that becoming an effective leader does *not* mean being cruel or in any way unfair. On the contrary, a good leader makes sure that no harm will come to his or her canine charges. Establishing yourself as the leader should *never* involve hitting or abusing your pet in any way. Remember, you want to help your dog behave properly, not scare her into submission.

Keep Your Dog Off the Bed and Other Furniture

The leader of a dog pack always desires the highest sleeping or resting area. Quite literally, the dog who sleeps highest gains the most power. If you allow your dog to sleep in bed with you or regularly rest in your favorite chair, you are telling him that he has equal status with you, the supposed leader.

The alpha male or leader of a wolf pack would never allow another adult pack member to co-opt his favorite, elevated sleeping spot. If another wolf attempted to do so, he would be reprimanded and chased away. If this did not happen, the invading wolf would gain leadership points, while the supposed leader would lose face.

Right from the start, provide your puppy or adult dog with a comfortable sleeping spot near to your own, but *physically lower* than your bed. Do the same with your favorite sitting areas: Allow your dog to rest near you, but not with or on you. In doing so, you will be telling him that you, the leader, have chosen these elevated spots as your own, per your rights as leader. Owners who mistakenly allow their dogs to sleep with them or rest on beds or easy chairs lose clout, leading to behavioral problems.

You can occasionally invite a *well-behaved* dog up onto your bed or chair if you want to, provided he gets down as soon as you say so. For dominant, pushy dogs, though, it is best to put a permanent stop to this habit. Doing so will remove one key area in which he mistakenly learns to vie with you as leader.

Walk Your Dog with a Relaxed Leash

Do you take your dog for a walk, or does she take you? Too often I see dogs dragging their hapless owners down the street, deciding where and how fast they will both go. This is an example of a dog literally leading the owner. If this scenario sounds familiar, you are losing leadership points.

You have to learn to walk your dog on a *relaxed leash*, with the dog at your side, willing to go where you want to go. Impossible? Not at all. A dog on a tight leash isn't paying attention to you, but is instead controlling the entire event. Think of a flock of geese flying overhead: Does their order change haphazardly, or remain stable? At the front of the triangular flight pattern is always the leader. That is how your dog thinks when she drags you down the street. She assumes the lead position over you.

A dog who walks by your side on the end of a loose leash is paying attention to you, and responding to where you are going. One of the very first things canine obedience classes teach is how to get your dog to do this. With the dog on the end of a six-foot leash (clipped to a training collar), instructors start with simply having their students stand in one spot while holding the end of the leash. If the dog begins to get to the end of the leash, the student simply administers a quick "pop" on the leash, while saying, "No, don't pull." Then, the dog is called over to the owner's side. The objective is to get the dog to understand that she must stay within a four- or five-foot radius of the owner. The "pop," or correction, is not painful, but is simply an attention getter or wake-up call. Once the dog learns to keep a loose relaxed leash while the owner is standing still, the instructor begins to have the students slowly walk back and forth around the room, continuing to enforce the "don't pull" command. Within a few days, the dogs in the class almost invariably learn not to pull.

To perfect this simple but important exercise, you will need to take an obedience class for beginners. These are widely available at any local humane society, or at local shelters and private canine-training facilities. The classes normally last six to eight weeks, and they will absolutely be the best step you can take in establishing yourself as a leader in your dog's eyes.

Waiting at the Door

Leaders instinctively go first, in all cases. This is the very definition of "leading." That said, when you open the door to take your dog for a walk, who goes normally out first? Not you, right? Mistake.

As the leader, you should make your dog wait at the door for a moment while you yourself step out. Then allow him to come through. This simple exercise is an extremely effective way to alter the dynamics for your little "pack." If practiced regularly, your pooch will slowly learn that you go first and he goes second. You will earn leadership points every time you go first, ahead of your dog.

Clip your dog's leash onto his training collar, and then prop open the door, or have someone open it for you. Have your dog sit, and then slowly lead him up to the open door. Have him sit again, right at the threshold, and do not allow him to go through. Tell him to "wait" (and include a hand sign such as an open palm), and then quietly and quickly step sideways across the threshold, while holding the leash up in the air and watching the dog. If your dog tries to step through with you, correct him with a quick, light pop on the leash (back toward the inside of the home), and tell him "wait" again. Keep practicing this until you can get the dog to wait at the threshold for a few seconds, with you on the other side of the entry. Then simply say "okay!" in a happy voice, allowing the dog through.

Eat Before Your Dog Does

The leader of a wolf pack always begins eating before the other adult members. A sign of privilege and respect, this "perk" clearly marks the leader as an important, powerful, admired individual. If another wolf had the audacity to challenge this feeding procedure, she would be confronted by the leader, who would most likely easily prevail.

If you intend to be a leader with your dog, you too will need to eat before your pet. Unfortunately, the average owner does the reverse. He or she comes home from work, greets and walks the dog, and then quickly feeds her. Only then does he or she begin to prepare the "human" dinner. The dog instinctively sees this as a sign that she is dominant, just as the alpha wolf would.

To correct this, simply feed your dog *after* you and your family eat. The object here is not to tease the dog, but to make her understand that you and the other humans in the "pack" are dominant over her. She will be fed, *after* you.

Do not under any circumstances allow your dog to beg while you eat. If she becomes noisy and animated while you are eating simply put her in another room. Sticking with this new feeding order will eventually help you take back some control and restructure the leadership hierarchy in the home. By doing so, you will cut down on bad behavior and the need to use food as a distraction tool. You will slowly gain control through leadership and not bribery.

Control Space and Possessions

Many pushy dogs have a habit of commandeering certain areas of the home, such as a chair or a space beneath a table. They choose this spot to rest in, and object to sharing it with anyone (or anything) else. Often a dominant dog will actually growl or nip at a family member innocently trying to gain access to the area, or attempting to move the dog.

As leader, you must not allow your dog to take over any areas of your home. The only area your dog should have control over is his crate, or doghouse. That's it. So, if you have mistakenly allowed your pushy pooch to rest on your bed or easy chair, you will have to stop him from doing so. If your dog growls when you try to move him from an area you need to clean, you'll need to deal with that too. But how?

Simple: Keep a leash on the dog while in the home. If your dog finds his way onto your bed or chair, simply tell him, "No; off!" and then pick up the end of the leash and guide the pet down. Or, if he is lying under a table in a space you want to clean, simply say, "Come on!" or "Get!" while leading the dog out with the leash. *Never* grab the dog by his collar, as this could provoke an aggressive or fearful reaction. *Always* use your leash when attempting to control your dog. If your pooch is particularly dominant and stubborn, keeping a leash on him all the time while in the home will allow you to always win contests of wills, something that must be done if you are to gain leadership.

However, if your dog does show serious aggression toward you or your family members, *you must seek out professional help from a trained canine behaviorist.* Do not try to handle this yourself; you or the dog could get hurt. See your veterinarian for a reference.

You must also have unrestricted access to the objects in your home, especially those you consider your own. Many dominant pushy dogs steal pieces of clothing, portions of food, or other human possessions, and then play a "keep away" game or, in worst-case scenarios, show aggression when the rightful owner tries to reclaim the item. Other dogs will growl or bite when an owner tries to retrieve a dog toy, bone, or food dish. This is not appropriate behavior for a dog to show his supposed leader. In fact, any dog who does have this type of reaction plainly sees himself as the leader, and must therefore be properly trained.

If your dog steals your objects or growls at you when you try to take something away from him, fall back on the trusted leash. Keep it on the dog while in the home, and use it to guide the dog away from a prohibited item. At the same time, make sure to "dog-proof" the home: Pick up all tempting or loose items from within the dog's reach, just as you would do with a two-year-old child. *Do not attempt to take an object out of the mouth of an aggressive animal. Rather,* wait until he becomes bored with it before removing it, and then put it away permanently. *And see a canine behaviorist,*

ASAP. This type of behavior is not normal, and it should never be tolerated!

Control Interactions

As the leader, you should be in charge of greeting strangers. Unfortunately, most owners allow their dog to have that job. In doing so, they are unintentionally telling the dog that she is the boss.

From now on, you should greet strangers on the street or in your home before your dog does. Again, use the trusted leash to do this, or else just keep the dog away from the front door, in another room, on a leash tethered to a doorknob, or in a crate. If on the street, simply tell your dog "sit." Shake hands with the stranger, and *then* allow the stranger to greet your dog. If your dog wants to jump all over the person, simply lead her away and try again. Eventually the dog will understand that she only gets petted while sitting in a calm fashion. By taking control of greetings, you reduce her leadership points and increase your own. And, again, enroll in a local obedience class, to learn proper technique with the leash and training collar.

Remain Calm, Fair, and Confident

Above all, the leader of a wolf pack usually knows how to deal with any situation presented to him, from the mundane to the life-threatening. In addition, the leader never treats the other pack members unfairly, and he always remains brimming with confidence.

For your dog to be able to accept you as a leader, you need to be able to deal with any circumstance that arises, from the appearance of a strange dog to the treatment of an injury. If you panic, your dog will too, and you will lose credibility as a leader.

Whatever happens, remain calm and authoritative when with your dog. Be fair; don't take your frustrations out on the animal by yelling or hitting, and don't punish him for something that happened in the past. For punishment to be effective, you need to administer it *when the inappropriate behavior occurs.* You have to catch the dog in the act. Dogs live very much in the moment; if your pooch gets into the garbage at ten A.M. and you discover the mess at six P.M., any punishment you mete out then will not make any sense to the dog, who will simply think that he is being punished for lying in front of the door when you came home.

Remember, by becoming a leader in your dog's eyes, you will be gaining her respect and obedience. Once those key issues are established, your dog will be easier to control. You won't have to bribe her with treats, or give in to her demands for more food.

Leadership and Training for Cats

No, the above heading is not a typographical error. Cats can be trained, and, like dogs, they need to know their status in the home. Unlike dogs, however, cats are remarkably self-sufficient, and they need very little training to function perfectly in your home. They don't need to learn to perform tricks or any other basic obedience behavior, primarily because, well, they're cats. Part of the reason we love them so much is because of their independent, narcissistic nature. They are haughty and so full of themselves that we just can't resist them.

Improper behavior on a cat's part can occur, however,

and can indirectly lead to problems with feeding and, ultimately, obesity. Like dogs, cats can very quickly learn to beg or purposely misbehave to receive a food bribe. Fortunately, the variety of undesirable feline behaviors is much smaller than in dogs, as is the frequency. Cats really are much less work than dogs, especially during their early months.

Establishing Leadership with Your Cat

As stated earlier, cats do recognize a dominance hierarchy in the home, although it is not nearly as important—or well developed—to them as to dogs. The object of a cat owner should be to become, in the cat's eyes, a foster mother, and not a littermate. Kittens fight with littermates and compete with them for food, status, and attention. If your cat sees you as a sibling, he will assume the right to behave toward you in this fashion. Teaching a cat that you are his mother is not all that cut-and-dry, however, because every cat is an individual, with a repertoire of moods and behaviors that vary tremendously from cat to cat and moment to moment.

Try to encourage friendly, affectionate interactions with your cat, while discouraging displays of dominance or aggression, including scratching or biting. A kitten would never get away with showing overt aggression toward her mother, and you shouldn't let her either. If your cat ever does display aggression, rely on a spray bottle filled with water. Simply spraying the cat in the face whenever she gets out of hand will quickly teach her to avoid the inappropriate behavior. Try to establish this as early as possible, when the cat is under four months of age. While discouraging bad behaviors in this way, simultaneously praise and reward the cat for affectionate, appropriate interactions. Never grab an adult cat by the scruff to discipline her, as this could result in a bad scratching or biting incident. A kitten, however, can be firmly held in this fashion for a moment or two, to get your point across.

Don't ever force a cat to do something, or to accept petting or attention longer than he wants. Many cats will scratch or bite softly as a way to say, "Okay, that's enough now." Try to stop petting or playing with your cat *before* that stage is reached; stop when the cat is still happy and accepting of the activity. Also, allow the cat to decide when he wants to be stroked. Don't force affection at any time, but instead wait until the cat comes to you and seeks your affections. Having respect for a cat's personal boundaries will help you gain his respect, and will aid in establishing your "motherhood" status.

Always provide your cat with the essentials of life, as any parent would. An owner who neglects his or her cat's basic needs is certainly not going to win any "parent of the year" awards. Food, water, love, shelter, and protection from dangerous conditions are all mandatory provisions. If you neglect your cat, she will neglect you.

Basic Training: What to Expect from Your Cat

Your cat needs barely any training to get along well with you and your family. A few basics do need to be encouraged, however, for everyone to be happy.

First, all cats need to be able to use a litter box. Contrary to popular belief, this behavior is not totally instinctive. Kittens do have the innate urge to scratch in litter, but they have this behavior enforced and encouraged by watching their mothers and littermates do it. By the time your kitten comes home, she should have the behavior firmly in place, thank goodness! Nevertheless, you will need to show your kitten where the box is in the home. Initially, get down and actually paw at the litter yourself (just make sure it's clean first!). After that, simply keep the box as clean as possible, and change the litter every week. Scooping at least twice each day will help prevent accidents outside the box. Also, always try to use the same brand of litter, and keep the box in the same area of the home, as moving it could provoke an accident. Place the box in a quiet, low-traffic area.

Try to teach your cat to recognize her name. Doing so will expand the cat's intellect and help create a bond between you. Simply say the cat's name over and over while petting her, and also just as food is served.

Teach your cat to tolerate being in a travel crate, so that you will be able to transport her without fuss. Crate training will also make time spent in the veterinarian's waiting room a breeze. Starting this behavior when the cat is young makes it easier. Simply place the kitten in a travel crate that has a special treat inside. Leave the kitten in there for a few minutes, and then release. Gradually increase the time inside until your kitty can stay in there indefinitely, without fear.

Most training for cats simply involves teaching them boundaries, or what *not* to do. Keep your cat off certain pieces of furniture by closing doors, spraying the cat with water if she jumps up onto the piece, or placing double-sided sticky tape around all prohibited areas. Cats hate the sticky feel on their feet, and they will eventually learn to avoid those areas. After a few weeks you should be able to remove the tape. Sheets or strips of aluminum foil also work well and can be removed more quickly.

Don't let your cats eat your houseplants. In addition to being beautiful and valued, many of them can be toxic to your cat. Keep the plants in a closed-off room, or place double-sided sticky tape around them. Sprinkle the soil with a bit of black or cayenne pepper to prevent digging in the dirt, or else buy plastic covers for the pots, designed so that only the shoots or trunks of the plants fit through. These are available in well-stocked pet shops. Commercially available cat repellants are also available at most pet shops. If you see your cat attempting to eat a houseplant, use your spray bottle! When possible, hang a plant from the ceiling or place it on a pedestal. Do not have dieffenbachia, ivy, or philodendron in the home, as these are particularly toxic to cats. Outdoor plants such as tomato, azalea, mushroom, yew, bean, or rhododendron are also all very toxic to cats.

Your cat should never mark, or spray, inside your home, which is generally a behavior of tomcats (though possible with females as well). You can reduce the odds of it by having your cat spayed or castrated before sexual maturity. If your cat still marks indoors, take him to your veterinarian for an evaluation to rule out any medical problem. Then, whenever you catch him in the act, spray him with your water bottle. If the behavior persists, seek professional help from a feline behaviorist found through your veterinarian.

Remember, a well-behaved cat or dog is much less likely to beg or bully you into handing over treats and table scraps. In addition, the pet will be more pleasant to be around, and she will have less of a need to drown her troubles in the food dish. A well-behaved pet will ultimately be better equipped to understand that there is indeed life after food.

7. Stay Aware of Your Pet's Physical and Behavioral Conditions

Keeping a close eye on your pet's appearance, vital statistics, behavior, and overall mood can help prevent illness or unusual behavioral problems from occurring, thereby avoiding any profound changes in eating habits or overall metabolism, the two most important factors affecting your cat or dog's body weight.

Cats and dogs accept and tolerate pain and discomfort much more effectively than do humans. Rarely do they cry out or actively complain, unless the problem becomes very serious. Because of this, a pet's health can suffer a tremendous amount before his owner becomes aware of the problem.

Be Aware of Changes in Behavior

You need to become very observant and aware of your pet's behavior. When a dog or cat is ill, the first sign may not be physical change, but rather some change in behavior. For instance, if a dog has a gastrointestinal infection, you will most likely see an abrupt change in her elimination and feeding habits. The pet's house-training may deteriorate, and her appetite may fall off. A sick cat may become moody, and might isolate himself from the rest of the household, perhaps spending most of his time beneath a bed or in a dark quiet place. A normally gregarious, friendly pet may suddenly become antisocial or short-tempered when ill, or could take on unfamiliar behavior patterns such as chewing incessantly on herself or excessively vocalizing.

Behavioral Changes That Can Indicate a Medical Problem

- sudden change in appetite
- a change in the pet's level of sociability
- incessant scratching, chewing, vocalizing, pacing, or panting
- hiding away in a dark, quiet area of the home
- irritability, or uncharacteristic growling or biting
- a change in elimination habits
- increased water intake
- any new compulsive behavior
- a sudden onset of destructive behavior
- any sudden increase in territorial behavior
- altered sleep patterns
- an unwillingness to play or exercise

Physical Changes That Can Indicate a Medical Problem

- discharge from the eyes, ears, nose, mouth, penis, vulva, or anus
- excessively dry or greasy coat
- hair loss
- rashes, sores, or blisters

- limping or favoring a leg
- discomfort upon being touched
- excessive drooling
- excessively pale gums
- warm nose
- shivering
- a wobbly, unsteady gait
- difficulty breathing
- vomiting
- coughing or sneezing
- excessive shaking of the head
- unpleasant odor

If you notice any of these behavioral or physical changes in your cat or dog, or any other changes that last more than a few days, see your veterinarian as soon as possible. He or she will be able to diagnose the problem and most likely get your pet back into good health. Remember you can only attempt any type of dietary or behavioral modifications with a healthy pet. To do so with a sick pet could worsen a condition, or at the very least camouflage it.

Keep a Weekly Medical Log

Even when your dog or cat is perfectly healthy, try to keep a weekly log of his vital statistics. In addition to helping diagnose any hidden problems, this record will allow you to track any weight loss or gain. Measurements and observations to write down include:

- weight
- chest and stomach measurements
- resting pulse and respiration (see below)

- temperature (see below)
- condition of gums, teeth, and nails
- stool color and consistency
- color of urine
- overall appearance, behavior, and appetite

Have a rectal thermometer on hand in case your pet appears under the weather. For dogs and cats, normal body temperature should be 100.5 to 101.5 degrees Fahrenheit. To take a dog's temperature, first apply a thin coat of K-Y Jelly to the thermometer. Then lift your dog's tail up and gently insert the thermometer in his anus, being careful not to twist it. If necessary, have a friend help you keep the dog steady so that the instrument does not get broken. Keep in for two minutes, and then remove and read the results.

Taking a cat's temperature is not always an easy task. Cats just do not like that part of their bodies invaded. The technique is identical to that used on dogs, but it may require you to wear long gloves, or even wrap the cat up in a towel to prevent injury to yourself. If your cat is highly resistant, do not keep trying. Instead, let your vet take her temperature.

A dog's resting pulse rate can vary from 70 to 120 beats per minute, depending on his size. The easiest way to check the pulse rate is at the point where the inner part of the rear thigh meets the body. Place two or three fingers there and count the number of beats in a minute.

A cat's resting pulse rate can vary from 110 to 130 beats per minute, depending on size. Check your cat's pulse in the same manner you would a dog's.

A dog's respiratory rate can vary from 10 to 30 breaths per minute, depending on size. A cat's respiratory rate can vary from 20 to 30 breaths per minute, depending on size.

To measure this for either species, simply observe the pet closely while she rests in a comfortable position. Placing a hand lightly on the pet's chest will aid you in getting an accurate count.

Perform a Weekly Home Exam

Once each week, take the time to go over your pet's body, from head to tail. Doing so may help you catch a serious problem in the making, such as a growing tumor or an abscess. Get into the habit of checking the following:

- *Coat* should appear lustrous. A dry, greasy, or patchy coat could indicate a dietary deficiency, parasites, dehydration, fungal infection, or an allergic condition.

- *Skin* should be clear and pink. Dry skin could indicate dehydration, parasites, allergies, or a dietary deficiency. Crusted or scabbed areas could mean fleas, allergies, infection, or skin ulceration. Also look for bite marks, which could become infected.

- *Body* should be free from lumps or swelling. Any unusual lump or raised area could indicate a tumor or an infection. Your pet's stomach should not be swollen or excessively hard, conditions that could point to gastritis, bloat, or worm infestation. A swollen or distended bladder could indicate a urinary tract infection, or stones. Swollen lymph glands around the neck could mean infection or cancer.

- *Eyes, ears, nose, anus, and penis or vulva* should be free of abnormal discharge. The pet's nose should be moist and cool to the touch. Any unusual puslike secretions, waxy buildup, or blood could point to viral or bacterial infection, kidney or bladder problems, a trapped foreign body, parasitic infection, or impacted anal glands.

- *Feet and nails* should be free of any foreign objects such as thorns or slivers of wood. Overgrown nails could affect the pet's posture and gait, so keep him well-groomed.

Grooming

Make sure to brush long-haired pets each day, to prevent mats and dirt from building up. Try to begin this habit while the dog or cat is young, as many adult pets (especially cats) resist this type of contact. Shorthaired pets should be brushed at least once per week. Though cats do keep themselves quite clean, you should still brush them to reduce the formation of hairballs, stimulate normal skin secretions, and remove any potentially toxic contaminants that might have collected on their coats.

Bathe your pet only when she needs it, especially with a cat. Too frequent bathing will dry out your pet's skin and coat. If your dog or cat becomes infested with fleas or ticks, however, you will need to give her a bath, using a veterinarian-approved flea and tick shampoo. Make sure you thoroughly rinse the pet off afterward, to prevent soapy residue from collecting on the pet's hair.

Some pets will resist bathing. If your dog or cat is one of these pets, do not force the issue. Instead, take her to a qualified groomer, who will expertly clean your reticent companion.

The same goes for nails, which should be trimmed at least once each month on both dogs and cats. Trimming nails should be done with a well-made nail trimmer purchased at a pet shop. Only remove about one-eighth of an inch each time, to eliminate the chance of cutting the quick, a small vein inside the nail, which will bleed profusely if cut. If your pet is resistant (or if you don't think you have the confidence to try it), consider letting the groomer do the trimming.

Schedule a Yearly Checkup with Your Veterinarian

Perhaps the most important health-related move you can make is to take your dog or cat to the veterinarian at least once each year. This will help keep him healthy and might just save his life. In addition, your veterinarian will be able to give you sound advice on diet and exercise and will help determine how much weight your pet needs to lose.

Also, have your pet's teeth cleaned at least once every couple of years, to maintain good oral hygiene and preserve as many teeth as possible.

Conclusion

As you have read, preventing obesity in your dog or cat involves more than simply feeding less. It involves becoming aware of your pet's individual habits, unique dietary needs, physical capabilities, and environmental interaction, as well as *your own* lifestyle and habits, and how those directly affect your companion. Knowing your pet and yourself are the keys to helping your favorite pooch or kitty stay trim, fit, and happy. Realize that *you alone* are the choreographer; your pet depends on you for food, love, exercise, and other forms of stimulus necessary for a sound mind and body. The buck stops with you; you have accepted the role of pet owner, and it is one that requires care, leadership, authority, and common sense. Always realize that your cat or dog, regardless of how intuitive or physically capable, has the reasoning capacity of a *two-year-old child*, and simply cannot be allowed to make vital, life-affecting decisions. That should be your responsibility. You need to understand that your dog or cat is a complex, emotional, responsive, yet malleable creature who will quickly learn the right way or the wrong way to act, depending on your input. If you choose to neglect or spoil, your pet's behavior and physical appearance will reflect it. If you willingly take on the reins of owner responsibility, your dog or cat will enjoy a happier, healthier life, with you by her side.

The following are brief summaries of the seven key points to pet weight loss. Remember that all are important; neglecting one for another may result in a chink in the armor and allow your pet to gain weight.

1. *Identify the cause of your pet's obesity.* Schedule a visit with your veterinarian and keep a week-long record of exactly what (and when) your pet eats, as well as recording everything he does.

2. *Evaluate yourself* to see how you are contributing to the problem.

3. *Adapt your pet's eating habits* to better fit her metabolism and lifestyle.

4. *Exercise your pet* to accelerate metabolism, burn calories, and relieve boredom. Every pet has at least a few exercises that she can and will participate in joyfully.

5. *Establish behavioral enrichment programs* for your cat or dog to relieve boredom and stimulate his instincts and intelligence. In doing so, you will help your overweight pet live a more stimulating life, an essential ingredient in any pet weight loss program.

6. *Train your pet* in order to establish leadership and behavioral boundaries, which will in turn aid in stabilizing her food drive and create a confident, secure mind-set. A well-behaved and respectful pet will be less likely to abuse food privileges.

7. *Stay aware of your cat or dog's physical and behavioral conditions.* Catching medical or psychological problems before they become serious will help ensure a stable metabolism, one key to maintaining a healthy food drive.

Finally, make sure to find and use a caring, competent veterinarian, who will become one of the key players in the fight to reduce your pet's weight and keep him healthy for years to come. A careful, concerted effort by you, your veterinarian, and all involved family and friends will result in permanent weight loss for your loving, charismatic four-legged companion. You deserve good health, and so too does your furry little friend.

Appendix A

Caloric Values of Foods Used in Home Cooking for Dogs and Cats

Lightly Cooked Meats

1 cup lean beef	300 calories
1 cup white-meat chicken	260 calories
1 cup dark-meat chicken	300 calories
1 cup lamb	325 calories
1 cup white-meat turkey	280 calories
1 cup dark-meat turkey	325 calories

Cooked Grains

1 cup brown rice	200 calories
1 cup oats	180 calories
1 cup barley	200 calories
1 cup cornmeal	150 calories

Cooked Vegetables

1 cup green beans	40 calories
1 cup zucchini	45 calories
1 cup carrots	40 calories
1 cup broccoli	40 calories

Steve Duno

Cooked Legumes

1 cup kidney beans	200 calories
1 cup pinto beans	200 calories
1 cup soybeans	240 calories
1 cup lentils	175 calories
1 cup white beans	175 calories

Dairy

1 whole raw egg	75 calories
1 ounce cheddar cheese	115 calories
4 ounces cottage cheese	100 calories
4 ounces yogurt	110 calories

Appendix B

Home-Cooked Recipes for Dogs and Cats

Basic Recipe for Dogs

3 cups raw or lightly cooked ground meat (beef, chicken, turkey, or lamb)

3 cups cooked grains (oats, brown rice, barley, or cornmeal)

½ cup cooked vegetables (green beans, zucchini, carrots, or broccoli)

1 raw egg

1 teaspoon bonemeal

1 teaspoon olive oil

Mix all ingredients together, then let cool for 30 minutes.
Yield: About 7 cups, with approximately 250 calories per cup.
Daily ration: Feed according to daily caloric requirements listed in chapter 3.

Basic Recipe for Cats

4 cups raw or lightly cooked ground meat (beef, chicken, turkey, lamb, or fish)

1 cup cooked grains (oats, brown rice, barley, or cornmeal)

¼ cup cooked vegetables (green beans, zucchini, carrots, or broccoli)

1 raw egg

1 teaspoon bonemeal

1 teaspoon olive oil

Mix all ingredients together, then let cool for 30 minutes.
Yield: About 6 cups, with approximately 260 calories per cup.
Daily ration: Feed according to the daily caloric requirements listed in chapter 3.

Index

Index

Index